The War Dead of the Hull General Cemetery

Bill Longbone & Pete Lowden

© Bill Longbone & Pete Lowden 2018.

This book is dedicated to the memory of both Walter Gawthorpe and Michael Kelly. Two young men who marched away to war and never came back to their loved ones.

They gave their lives then for our future now.

Contents:

Introduction	7
Preface	8
Section One	10
Section Two	66
Appendices	112
Bibliography	124

Acknowledgements:

Figs 1,2,3: **The Story of 25 Eventful Years in Pictures**, Odhams Press

Figs 4,5,7,8,9,10,31,34: Authors' own postcards.

Fig 6: **British and Commonwealth War Cemeteries**, Julie Summers, Shire,

Figs 11,12,13,23,24,25,26,27,28,29,30,33,35,36,37,38,44,45,52,69,80: Hull Daily Mail.

Figs 14,15,16,17,18,19,20,21,32,39,40,42,43,47,48,49,50,53,54,58,61,64,65,66,67,70,72,73,74, 75,78: Authors' own photographs.

Figs 22,59,62: Hull, The Good Old Days, Facebook site.

Figs 41,56,57,59,60,63,71,81: The National Archives

Figs 46,47: George Heber

Figs 51,55: Hull History Centre

Figs 76,77,79: Nadine Tull

Appendix 1: Imperial War Graves Commission booklet regarding war grave burials in Hull; section devoted to Hull General Cemetery.

Appendix 2: As above but marked by staff at Commonwealth War Graves Commission. Please note comments of 'unmaintainable'.

Appendix 3: Correspondence between Hull General Cemetery and IWGC in 1917. History Centre.

Appendix 4: Spreadsheet of Hull General Cemetery known war graves. Thanks to Bill.

Appendix 5: Maps of Hull General Cemetery with approximate war grave locations. Thanks to Bill.

Obviously, we'd like to thank everyone who always attempts to steer us in the right direction and who smile at our poor jokes. These include, The Carnegie Heritage Centre, Hull History Centre, Kingston upon Hull War Memorials website, The Commonwealth War Graves Commission, the 'Hull: The Good Old Days' website and an especial thank you to Nadine Tull for allowing precious photographs of her family, the Margerisons, to be used by us in this project.

Also, to Jeanne and Barbara who respectively live with two old men who feel that a good day out is seeing an interesting headstone.

Of course, it goes without saying that any mistakes are unintentional. Be that as it may, both Bill and I claim all responsibilities for any and all of them.

Introduction

This book, like our last one, is a collaborative effort by both Bill and myself. We endeavour to share the workload, be that researching, planning, writing, and laying the work out, or any of the other maddening little details that can hinder your ideas getting into print.

The book itself is divided into sections; the first section deals with the problems that beset the forces of the British Empire with the burying of their fallen during the Great War of 1914-18. It then highlights how the issue was solved by the formation of the Imperial War Grave Commission (now the Commonwealth War Grave Commission) whilst the fighting was still continuing. The formulation of the main principles it adopted, and that still govern its work, is discussed. The book then moves on to record how this organization achieved the goals that they had set themselves, and the difficulties that they had to overcome to do so.

The wider issue of remembrance of the fallen, and how they were memorialised after the Great War, is also discussed with an emphasis upon Hull. Finally, the story of how Hull General Cemetery 'lost' its War Grave Headstones is explained.

The second section looks at those individuals who occupy the grave spaces that once were commemorated with a War Grave headstone, and who are still buried in Hull General Cemetery. This section chronicles their lives, pitifully short in some cases, and how they met their death. It is complemented, where possible, by a number of illustrations that allow the reader to put a face to these names and numbers, to allow that person to stand in the light once again.

The War Graves of Hull General Cemetery, compiled in this book, is as comprehensive a list of the fallen as we believe is possible given the length of time since their interment. We also include some other forces personnel who fell in these conflicts, but are remembered on family headstones within the cemetery, although their actual burial sites are on the continent.

Once again, all proceeds that this book earns goes to the Friends of Hull General Cemetery group, a subsidiary part of the Hull Civic Society.

Preface

When I was studying for my BA, as part of the final year, there was a component of English Literature. No problem, I thought. However, the 'rules' for the award of the degree, were that you should show evidence of familiarity with the three genres of the subject.

Now I'm fine with drama and prose but poetry has always left me cold, even at school. I could never see the point in hiding what you were trying to say to the audience in metaphor and imagery. I thought, and still do to some extent, Philistine that I am, that poetry was confusing its message by using language as a means of obfuscation rather than clarification. So, I was in a bit of a dilemma all those years ago.

I quickly discarded Byron, Shelley and many others. Things were getting tight. Looking down the next series of lectures, and the reading list, I noticed that later in the year it was to be Ted Hughes, Phillip Larkin and Sylvia Plath. Oh, good grief, I needed some help. Hello, what's this? First World War Poetry. Well I'd studied The Great War so I took a look.

The first few poets were, to my untutored ears, just as bad as the Romantic Poets. Rupert Brooke et al, said nothing to me. And then I chanced upon Siegfried Sassoon. Here was a man who didn't hide nor couch his meaning under flowery metaphor. No 'little piece of England in a foreign field' for him but images of limp bodies hung on barbed wire; rats as big as puppies feeding on corpses in flooded trenches; lice ridden, exhausted soldiers trooping up to the front knowing that they were soon to become Headquarters' next lot of cannon fodder. This was the truth, the reality for the soldiers of the Great War, and he chronicled it.

Needless to say, my issue with poetry was solved, for the purposes of the degree. I later discovered other poets of the period, who also recorded faithfully the sordid reality of the 'glory' of trench warfare that earlier poets had misrepresented, but none touched me on that visceral level like Sassoon had done.

In a poem, entitled **Aftermath**, written in 1919, when debates were raging about how best the dead of the Great War should be remembered, and the Imperial War Grave Commission was quietly going about its job of burying the fallen, Sassoon wrote this.

'Have you forgotten yet?

Look up and swear by the green of spring that you'll never forget.'

Up The Line To Death, Ed. Brian Gardner, Magnum, 1980.

We hope that this book will, hopefully, allow some of the forgotten war dead of Hull, in Hull's forgotten cemetery, to be remembered once again, and show that we haven't forgotten.

Pete Lowden & Bill Longbone

Section One

The guns of the Great War fell silent at 11.00 a.m. on November 11th 1918 but the dying didn't stop then. The United Kingdom had lost over half a million of its citizens, many of whom died in combat. Almost as bad, many armed forces personnel were hospitalised from wounds received whilst the conflict was still raging. Some would recover to a greater or lesser degree and return back into society. A smaller number, however, would die from their injuries, sometimes after a period of suffering for years. Another portion of the British forces would die as the result of the Influenza pandemic of 1918-19 whilst still enrolled in the forces. All of these individuals were entitled to burial within a War Grave, as defined by the Imperial War Grave Commission, even though it could be argued they had not died in battle.

The vast majority of those war graves are situated overseas, and by far the vast majority of those may be found in France and Belgium. If you have ever visited such sites, as both of the authors have, one cannot help but be shocked at the slaughter that must have taken place to produce so many headstones, marching in line after line to the horizon. Apart from the sheer emotional impact of the sites, one also cannot help but admire the loveliness and beauty that such sites were designed to convey to the visitor. This setting was no accident. It was arrived at by design and much careful thought.

The same principles that shaped the war grave cemeteries of Europe were also applied to the armed forces personnel who died in Britain and were buried in their local cemeteries. Obviously, the long-serried lines of headstones could not be emulated, but the same type of headstone was used, the same lettering was employed on the headstone and the headstone was placed so it was the same height above ground as the ones in Europe. In this way the person lost could be remembered as one of the many war dead, but they could also be accommodated in the family grave or the local cemetery.

For those of us who visit cemeteries regularly, the war grave headstones are ubiquitous, and, especially in Victorian cemeteries, may appear nondescript and plain against the huge memorials standing near them, but, in that almost simple and sparse way, the headstones assume more gravity and respect than the grandest of obelisks next to it. In achieving this emotional response, the headstone captures the aims set out by the founders of the Imperial War Grave Commission all those years ago. Here is that story.

By the end of the Great War, the United Kingdom had lost at least 723,000 of its citizens, excluding the forces from the rest of the British Empire. [1] Some of these would have died in field hospitals close to the front and were buried in cemetery land, donated by the French and Belgian authorities. [2] Others unfortunately died whilst in transport back home to Britain, still others died in Britain, within the medical establishments set up to cater for the wounded. [3]

However, by far the largest percentage of the total casualties would have died at the front, and more than likely have been buried in field cemeteries, almost certainly sited just behind the front lines.

Another proportion of the total casualties would have been killed with no remains left for burial. Artillery was the usual culprit here, but others killed could have been buried so deeply from the constant shelling that the recovery of any remains would have been impossible. Most of these casualties, unless actually seen by, and reported as such by witnesses as having died, would have been listed as 'Missing in Action' or 'Missing, presumed dead'. This presumption of death was usually accurate.

An example of this type of casualty is Rudyard Kipling's son Jack. Jack had tried to enlist on his 17th birthday, but had been refused on medical grounds due to poor eyesight. His father used his influence to allow him to enlist. Four weeks later he was on his way to France and six weeks later he was listed as 'Missing' during the battle at Loos in 1915.[4] His body was never found. Only well after the

---

[1] p.544, Stevenson. The figure for deaths appears to be always rising as evidenced by the Commonwealth War Graves Commission Annual Report, the most recent, 2015, stating a figure in excess of 888,000 for the Great War.

[2] p.45, Gibson & Ward. (1989) The concept of *sepulture perpetuelle* is explained here. Pp.11-12 & 21-22, Longworth with regard to France and Belgium respectively. P.463, Laqueur.

[3] p.212, Bilton, **The Trench**. Many of the forces' personnel buried in Hull General Cemetery fall into this bracket.

[4] 'The first day of Loos had been costly in human life, and in young life too. It is known that at least eighty-six boys aged seventeen and under were killed that day.' p.157, Van Emden, **Boy Soldiers of the Great War**. P.37, Belley.

death of his parents, in 1986, were his remains identified and buried under a named headstone.[5]

Kipling wrote a short poem in 1916 a year after his loss, of which the first verse is written below. It perhaps comes closest to expressing the plight and pain of those left behind, in the limbo of not knowing what had happened to their loved ones.

> 'Have you news of my boy Jack?
>
> *Not this tide*
>
> When do you think that he'll come back?
>
> *Not with this wind blowing....* [6]

A recent film production, written by and starring David Haigh, (alongside Daniel Radcliffe, Kim Cattrall and Carey Mulligan), attempted to show how this one, admittedly upper-class family, tried to cope with their loss. It is now a successful stage play. The Kipling family's plight would be multiplied a thousand-fold.

Indeed, Kipling experienced this distress, vicariously, before he had lost his own son, when his friend, Lady Violet Cecil, lost her son, George, in the first few weeks of the war.[7] It was this incomprehension that the person who had walked out of the door in the soldier or sailor uniform, in their prime, would never be seen again. A terrible enough thought. To compound that loss by not knowing what had happened to them, whether they had died, quickly or slowly, or survived in some way, was almost more than could be borne. The juxtaposition between the smiling 'cheerio', at the door or the railway station as they left with their kitbag over their shoulder, and then the vast empty silence of years stretching ahead, must have been terrible to endure.

The story of Emily Chitticks, and her soldier fiancé, Will Martin, is a case in point. He enlisted in 1916, and whilst at the front he wrote 75 letters to her, and she sent him 23 back. Five of hers were returned to her with the single word 'Killed'

---

[5] p.180, Crane.

[6] Ibid.

[7] pp.38-47, Jalland. A concise description of one person's highly influential attempt to find out what had happened to her child and her subsequent failure. How much harder that must have been for the vast majority of the bereaved goes without saying.

inscribed upon them. She wanted to know the exact circumstances of how her fiancé died, and enquired of both his comrades, and the newly emerging Imperial War Graves Commission (IWGC) for further information. The Grave Registration Unit passed what information it knew to her, which eventually allowed her to place his death at close to 'S.E. of Arras' but no further. The piece of land her fiancé died upon, was fought over for the four years of the war, and his burial place was destroyed many times.

> 'In 1921, she collected Will's letters into a bundle to which she added a chronology of their relationship, a pencilled verse about how she won't see him on earth again, and a couplet in ink that read, "Sleep darling sleep, on foreign shore/ I loved and love you dearly, but Jesus loves you more." There is also a note saying that she wanted the packet buried with her, just as her heart was already buried in Flanders' Field. Her life, she said, had ended with his. Emily Chitticks never married and died alone in a council estate. She left no known heirs." [8]

Sad though this tale is, it must have become fairly commonplace the longer the conflict continued, although that does not make it any less bitter for the participants, nor for us who read such tragedies with the hindsight of history.[9]

The dual problem, outlined above, of not knowing where your loved one had died, nor having any remains that could be buried and visited, was one of the factors in the idea of creating the Tomb of the Unknown Warrior in Westminster Abbey, and also of the large memorials in IWGC cemeteries, subsequently erected after the war had ended, in France and Belgium where the names of the missing would be inscribed. The public embraced both concepts fiercely.[10]

> 'Commemoration of lost soldier sons became even more significant when bodies were never found, identified or buried, and so a new form of national civic memorial was required, to mourn the dead rather than celebrate war. This help explains the immense popular appeal of the

---

[8] pp.398-399, Laqueur.

[9] The most detailed account of this situation may be found in Nicholson.

[10] pp.480-482, Laqueur.

Cenotaph, the tomb of the Unknown Soldier (sic) and the ritual of Armistice Day.'[11]

Fig.1. The crowd passing the tomb of the Unknown Warrior at its opening on November 11th 1920.

---

[11] pp.252-253, Jupp and Gittings.

Fig.2. The Tomb of the Unknown Warrior, November 11th 1920.

C.F.G.Masterman, the Liberal politician, noted at the time of the burial of the Unknown Warrior that, 'we were burying every boy's father, and every woman's lover and every mother's child.' It gave solace to a grieving nation. It was said that more than a million and a quarter people filed past the tomb when it was first opened to the public.[12]

The laying of wreaths at the Cenotaph, once it became a permanent fixture and was erected in Whitehall in 1920, and of the local ceremonies taking place at

---

[12] p.481, Laqueur. pp.334-335, David Barnes.

their respective memorials to the fallen, added to the somber majesty that the nation felt befitted the ceremony, and their collective loss.[13]

This was the public face of death. This was commemoration of the loss of a nation's youth in mass. Although it could assuage some of the grief it could not touch the inner personal loss. To heal that hurt, one needed to see one's loved one's name on the memorial. One hoped for a trace of that tangibility, that essence of the person that had been stolen by the war. Can you imagine that this outpouring of grief surrounding the Armistice Day, the laying of the wreaths at the Cenotaph, or the burial of the Unknown Warrior, would have filled the empty space in Emily Chitticks, Violet West or Rudyard Kipling's lives? These rituals helped but they did not heal. As Jalland points out, in relation to another family suffering this loss,

> 'The primary source of consolation for the Bickersteths, as for many others, was not a state memorial in their homeland, but the spot in France where Morris's body was presumed to be buried.[14]

As a result of this, 'primal scream', being recognized by the authorities, and through the intelligence and foresight of one man, these survivors of grief and sorrow would have their needs met, and the instrument by which this occurred was the Imperial War Grave Commission.

The first battles of the Great War on the Western Front were fluid, with the German Army advancing and pushing the Allied forces from their original start lines back in to France. Occasionally the Allied forces stopped their retreat, and a fierce fire fight took place, such as at Mons. However, the overwhelming power of the German forces at that time, meant that the Allied forces had to continue their retreat until they reached the River Marne in the first weeks of September 1914.[15]

There, with a well-planned counter attack, against an overstretched right wing of the oncoming German Army, the Allied forces pushed the enemy back to the River Aisne. Here, the war stagnated into the trench warfare that people now,

---

[13] pp.234-235, Arthur, **The Road Home**, provides a markedly different view of how some of the comrades who survived the conflict believed how the dead should be remembered. More in celebration than in sorrow. Also p.328, Strachan cites similar views.

[14] p.68, Jalland.

[15] pp.78-96, Liddell Hart.

recognize as typical of the Great War. The next four years, saw minor changes in the front-line taking place, but at a tremendous cost in lives for both sides.

Fig.3. The laying of the wreaths at the commemoration of the permanent Cenotaph, 'the empty tomb', designed by Lutyens and finished in 1920. This photograph is of November 11th 1920.

Obviously, when the Allied forces were being pushed back into France, the dead were left on the battlefield, and the German forces buried them, collecting the necessary items that identified the corpses, and informing the Allied authorities of the details. These burial cemeteries were not disturbed until the final Allied push in the final months of the war, and even then, only slightly as the German Army retreated so quickly. The same occurred in the area around the Marne, where the Allied forces buried the fallen German forces' personnel in burial grounds. After 1914, these burial places were never disturbed until after the conflict had finished, when some bodies were repatriated at the request of the families.

Where problems occurred, with the burial of the fallen, was in the area that was to constitute the front line over the next four years. Attack and counter-attack lead to many people dying and falling in disputed territory.[16] Often both sides allowed the recovery of the bodies by burial parties. Sometimes they didn't. The bodies not recovered would become part of the landscape, eventually being buried and reburied accidentally, sometimes by the conflict going on around them, as and when circumstances dictated.

> 'There was little movement, as soldiers built or rebuilt trenches, they could hardly dig without discovering the remains of their countrymen or enemies.'[17]

Such bodies, when recovered, would however, be buried within a few miles of the front line, as transportation to sites further away was not deemed important enough, in contrast to using the transport for reinforcements, ammunition, food, medical supplies etc. As such these burial places were within the range of both sides' artillery and, although not specifically targeted, could well be disturbed, if not destroyed, by the blanket barrages common during this period of the war. If this happened, then the carefully buried bodies could be destroyed or so damaged that reburial would simply have been collecting up all of the remains in a communal grave.

Coupled with this aspect, was the effect that the artillery barrages could have upon the living. There are many veterans' recollections of seeing their comrades being blown to bits, or even of having them disappear completely when a shell

---

[16] P.296-297 Lewis-Stempel

[17] p.465, Laqueur.

achieved a direct hit. The problems of burial in such cases can scarcely be imagined.[18]

> 'Moved into the trenches where Lieutenant Kidder, Prvt. Coombs and White were blown to bits. We gathered their remains in sand bags and buried them 25-5-17'[19]

As discussed earlier, many of these cases would be listed as Missing, yet there was never any doubt amongst that person's comrades that they were dead, even though a body could not be produced. As George White, a 15-year-old soldier of the front line on burial duty, described after finding some bodies,

> 'We were conscious of the fact that by handing in the discs and pay-book of each man, his next-of-kin, who had probably been informed that he was missing and hoped he had been taken prisoner, would now receive the dreaded telegram informing them that he had been killed in action.'[20]

Of course, if that pay-book or identity disc were missing, then the lingering agony of that man's family would continue until, hopefully some identification took place, or more usually the man's family died, and all memory of him as a living person was extinguished. The man's existence as a living person having been lost, it became more important to remember them in a more permanent way, and in this the IWGC took on that task.

The problems were not just related to the identification of the soldier who had been killed. Problems arose even after burial as we have seen already in the case of Emily Chittick's fiancé when the burial site is hit by enemy fire. That this wasn't an isolated incident is obvious.

> 'Several crosses were lying about anyhow – these, if originally marking graves, had been blown from the spot they were intended to mark. I only noticed one cemetery which had been knocked about by shells and this one had suffered badly; the headstones being scattered about the place.'[21]

---

[18] 'Often when we moved in the trenches you trod and slipped on rotting flesh', p.465, Laqueur.

[19] p.465, Laqueur.

[20] p.75, Van Emden, Boy Soldiers of the Great War.

[21] p.375, Van Emden, **The Soldier's War**.

Fig.4. The idealised scene of the wartime burial for home consumption.

Fig.5. World War One Postcard, Daily Mail Series. Probably sanitised but slightly more realistic than the previous image.

Into this carnage stepped Fabian Ware. A retired editor of the Morning Post, and staunch Conservative and Imperialist, he was 45 years old at the outbreak of the war. He knew his chances of seeing action as a soldier would be limited, so he volunteered, and was taken on to be the commander of the Mobile Unit of the Red Cross. Arriving in France in September 1914 he quickly realised that, in time, a reckoning would be called on the authorities, as to the whereabouts of the British dead, by the fallen's families and society as a whole.[22] The Red Cross unit was probably best placed to record such details, and accordingly Fabian Ware made it one of their core tasks.

This role, of cataloguing the fallen dead, was unique in the history of the British Army as, in previous wars, the dead had fallen, and when the storm of war had passed, they were buried in mass graves with no fuss or memorialisation. In some instances, the bones of the dead were used as fertiliser for the local community. Indicative perhaps of a change in society as a whole, the much maligned, 'scum of the earth', the '1/- a day' soldier of the 19th century was

---

[22] p.62, Jalland. Ware's epiphany appears to have been his search for a fallen friend's grave in Bethune's local cemetery.

transformed into the citizen soldier, fulfilling a patriotic duty, and it was felt that they should be accorded respect and dignity in death.

Playing his hand very carefully, Ware managed to gain acceptance from, firstly the British Army command, and then the War Office, to acknowledge his unit's role in the identification and burial of the war dead.[23] By March of 1915, his unit was officially given this task with a new title of 'Graves Registration Commission'. This appointment gave official recognition of the work Ware's unit had been doing since the previous October. With the losses at Arras and Loos in 1915 showing that the task for the unit was becoming more burdensome, the unit was integrated within the British Army in September 1915.

Ware showed further foresight when he began to negotiate with the French authorities for land to be used as cemeteries for the fallen. The local cemeteries near the front lines would quickly have been overwhelmed by the carnage of the conflict. Although these negotiations were amicable, not least due to Ware's excellent French, and the principles of such transfers of land were quickly agreed, the final decision took some time to pass the French Senate. Ware realized that one of the sticking points was that, in a fit of generosity from the French, the first Bill would not only provide the land 'in perpetuity' but also the maintenance of the sites. In his further negotiations he suggested that the maintenance should be shared by the combatant nations and with this subtle change the necessary legislation was passed.[24]

As discussed above, the sheer immensity of locating all of the burial spaces, and all of the interments of the buried soldiers, was quickly grasped as probably not achievable. From 1916, the Graves Registration Unit, (GRU) the forerunner to the IWGC, began to establish burial grounds under their authority and the re-interment of the fallen began to take place in a more systematic way than had gone before.[25]

The initial burial of the war dead was the responsibility of the Army but the GRU took on the task of exhumation where the bodies could be moved to a more

---

[23] p.44, Gibson & Ward.

[24] p. 12, Longworth.

[25] pp.62-63, Jalland.

secure burial place, and buried with more formality than they had been earlier.[26] During this exhumation process it also was hoped to correctly identify

Fig.6. An example, showing not only the conditions the soldiers had to endure in the trenches (washing themselves in a shell hole), but also that the shell hole, part of a wartime cemetery, could be damaged by artillery fire.

---

[26] pp137-139, Van Emden, **The Quick and the Dead**.

Fig.7. Probably a more realistic image of a front-line burial, this one is French.

Fig.8. Daily Mail Series. Note the wooden crosses in the left background. Those were the more standard memorials used initially by the IWGC.

the bodies and register that identity of the body,

> 'A temporary wooden cross was erected above the grave and inscribed with the religion, regimental number, rank, name, unit and date of death.'[27]

In this way the GRU was essentially preparing the ground for how the war dead would be cared for after the conflict had ended. At that point it was not clear whether the war dead would be allowed to remain buried on the battlefield, or whether the families would want their relatives exhumed and brought back to Britain for burial. What it was doing was registering the buried soldiers' whereabouts and hopefully covering whatever eventualities the future might hold.

Fig.9. A British Cemetery on the Western Front dated around the end of 1919.

---

[27] p.24, Summers.

Fig.10. Close up of one of the styles of wooden crosses used in a typical British cemetery before the headstone was placed.

This was one of the most important factors that Ware recognised immediately. If their families repatriated the war dead, for reburial in Britain, this would leave many who could not afford the expense of such a move, having to leave their loved ones buried in France and Belgium. He felt this would negate the active feeling that all who served, whatever class or rank, were contributing equally in the struggle, and the idea of allowing class and wealth to subvert this sacrifice would cause antagonism. He gained acceptance of this stance from the Army in

April 1915, who stopped all exhumations on the grounds of hygiene.[28] Ware realized that this was only a stop-gap measure and he knew a greater fight lay ahead not just on exhumation, but on the principle of equality of headstone too.

The culmination of the issue was finally resolved, at least legislatively, after an acrimonious debate in the House of Commons. In this debate, seemingly on the proposed reduction to £5 from the £10 figure that Ware had suggested initially, as the cost of each individual headstone, albeit without him having any idea of the true cost, the principle of equality was finally ratified. Of course, the debate continued outside of Parliament.

The parliamentary debate was recorded in the Hull Daily Mail of the 5th of May 1920 under the headline, 'The Graves of Heroes', although it had made its feelings quite clear in an editorial of the 2nd of December 1918, stating that,

> 'Unquestionably it is better that the heroes who sleep in scattered and isolated graves where they fell in action should be gathered together in war cemeteries, and beyond doubt the exceptional desire to exhume and transport home should be discouraged.'[29]

The most articulate supporter of the amendment, to exhume the dead and bring the bodied home who could afford to, was not the original proposer, but Lord Robert Cecil, whose wife, Violet, mentioned earlier, had lost a son in the war. According to the Hull Daily Mail, he,

> 'Denied that this was a question of between rich and poor. The question was whether the tombstone placed over the original grave should be a national or personal monument.'[30]

However, a new spirit was in the air, even in the House of Commons where privilege was second nature, the sacrifice of so many men, and the idea that

---

[28] p. 45, Gibson & Ward. Ware was accused of being a socialist for taking this stance. 'The right of the next of kin had been abrogated by a secret treaty with a foreign power' and the House of Commons had been 'captivated by the socialist ideal'. P.471, Laqueur. That the Countess of Selborne wrote the above is a fact that in itself probably argued the case in Ware's favour more than he ever could.

[29] Hull Daily Mail, 2nd December 1918.

[30] Hull Daily Mail, 5th May 1920.

each and every one of those sacrifices should be treated with equal dignity, was upheld.

> 'The argument that prevailed at the House – that 'what is done for one should be done for all' made by William Burdetts' Coutts...stands in stark opposition to the aristocratic principle that had dominated the remembrance of the dead of war since Agincourt and that was eroding in the late nineteenth century.'[31]

The downside to this position was that if the family wanted to mourn their loved one at their grave they must travel to either France or Belgium.[32]

Of local interest here, relating to the issue of exhumation, is the case of Frank Foster Baron. Frank's father, Herbert H., was employed at Reckitts in the 'Blue & Starch' works. He must have been a reliable employee, because he and his family were living in Lilac Avenue, in Garden Village, at the time of the 1911 census.

At the time of this census, Herbert and his wife Annie, had only two children still living at home with them. These were Fred, 17 years old, a railway coal clerk and Frank Foster, 15 years old, a telegraph messenger boy. Annie had borne eight children of which five were still living. In 1901, the family had been living in St Mark's Street in the Groves, and the house contained as well as the above, two more daughters, Ada and Edith, but also the eldest boy, Herbert, aged 14, and already at work packing boxes, probably at Reckitts.

Herbert enlisted as a gunner in the Royal Field Artillery Regiment, in the May of 1914, and was posted overseas to France, in the September of that year. In the February of 1915 he was appointed Acting Saddler, later to become Saddler, in 1916.

Herbert survived the war, and later claimed a war service pension, but this was denied, as his injuries were that his teeth were rotten and needed to be extracted, which the authorities medical section felt hardly constituted a war

---

[31] p.472. Laqueur.

[32] Obviously, there were many other IGWC sites around the world set up in this period. Important and impressive Great War ones includes Salonika, the Dardanelles and Kut. However, to travel to such sites was usually well beyond the means of the average family in the inter-war period, a period of political uncertainty and economic austerity.

wound. After the war, Herbert set himself up in a saddle business, but with the advent of the motorcar, this was the wrong place and time for such a venture and he was cited as bankrupt in 1925. Eventually, he worked at Blackburn's Aircraft factory, making seats for airplanes, where his saddlery skills would have been useful. He died in Hull in 1962.

His younger brother Frank Foster, who was 15 in 1911, enlisted in 1915, in the same regiment as his elder brother as a gunner. Frank fought through the war until he was killed in France in the September of 1918, and was buried there. Richard Van Emden, in **The Quick and the Dead**, found a supplemental part to this story that must have been published in the local newspapers in Belgium, if at all.

Van Emden states that Herbert took 20 months to prepare for this expedition, and its goal was simply to exhume his brother's body, and bring it back home to Hull for burial. Apparently, he had reached the point of actually being in the Belgian cemetery, and on the point of disinterring his brother's body, when a local gendarme, who must have been somewhat surprised at what he saw, discovered him and took him into custody. The expedition was foiled.

How he intended to get his brother's body back across the channel and then to Hull may well have been parts of his plan not that well thought out. As for where it would have been buried once it was returned to Hull, this may also have been sketchily planned.

We have no knowledge of how the authorities dealt with Herbert, we hope that it was with some leniency, but it is an example of the depths of emotion that swirled around the issue of burial in war cemeteries at that time.[33]

Those who did make the effort, and could afford the expense, often found the residue of war rather than the neatly tended grave they hoped to find. Sir Edward Poulton visited his son Ronald's grave,

> 'The Cemetery, which had been fought over, bore many scars of the war [with] craters filled with water and trees splintered and broken off. The fence and rustic gateway put up had disappeared. Ronald's grave was

---

[33] pp.280-281, Van Emden, **The Quick and the Dead.**

uninjured, although there were four shell holes within a few feet of it; the oak cross was intact except from two shell splinters."[34]

However, on the whole, the local staff recruited by the IWGC attempted to make the destination, if not the journey, have a more satisfactory outcome than Sir Edward Poulton's.[35]

Although concerns were raised that the poorer families would not be able to afford the journey to visit their loved ones' graves, even with the subsidy that the government allowed to the families to help with the expenses that such a visit would incur, this was not the case.[36]

> 'To give an idea of the numbers travelling, the Church Army took 5000 family members in the months to June 1919, the Salvation Army another 18,500 between 1920 and 1923, while the YMCA helped 60,000 between 1919 and 1923.'[37]

This issue surfaced in the Hull Daily Mail too.

---

[34] p.285. Van Emden, **The Quick and the Dead**.

[35] pp.86-91, Max Arthur, **The Road Home**.

[36] pp.256-259, Van Emden, **The Quick and the Dead**.

[37] p.287. Van Emden, **The Quick and the Dead**.

VISITS TO WAR GRAVES.

BETTER FACILITIES BY AUTUMN.

Questions continue to be addressed to Ministers, says a Parliamentary correspondent, asking for facilities for relatives to visit the graves of their dead in France and Flanders.

It may be as well to explain that there are almost insuperable difficulties in the way of such visits at present. There are no restrictions imposed by the War Office, and the Foreign Office issues passports in the usual way, but there is no organisation on the other side for getting about. Those who are fortunate enough to find a private motor car may reach their destination, but such opportunities are rare. It is, moreover, the fact that in many places the military authorities have found it necessary to exhume and reinter bodies, and the cemeteries concerned are closed in the meantime.

This circumstance, and the fact that the War Office hopes to provide facilities in the autumn for visits under conditions of organised convenience, may induce those who are naturally anxious to make the journey as early as possible to postpone the intention until these facilities can be provided.

Fig.11. Hull Daily Mail, 15th May 1919.

Suffice to say that by the early 1920's the cemeteries were, as envisaged by Ware and the rest of his committee,

> 'Like oases in a barren landscape, with lawns gradually covering the mud, and flowers and bushes and rapidly growing saplings planted among the graves.'[38]

---

[38] p.292. Van Emden, **The Quick and the Dead**.

Surprisingly this wasn't to everyone's taste.

> 'It has been a terrible disappointment. This war is gone for ever – only a memory now. What we last saw as a vast desert of shell holes, bare tree stumps, mud, filth, smashed guns and tanks and dead men, is all waving cornfield, pretty gardens, brand new villages, noisy estaminets, charabancs, quarrelling children, and flight girls. It makes one's heart thump. The only things left to remind one that memories once were immense realities are the cemeteries and the poppies.'[39]

Again, some people, probably due to their unfamiliarity with their foreign surroundings, acted in an unseemly manner, lighting fires and cooking meals within the cemeteries.[40]

This became such an issue that a letter from Rudyard Kipling was published in every newspaper to highlight this issue.

The uniform headstone that was adopted by the IWGC for use in its cemeteries, and also in municipal cemeteries across Britain was, as already mentioned, another battle that the IWGC had to fight concurrently with the exhumation issue.

Like the 'aristocratic principle' mentioned above, a number of people felt that they wanted to memorialise their family member in their own way. This usually meant via a tomb or monument, in much the same way as they probably would have done at home in Britain, in their local cemetery or churchyard. To Ware, this prospect was an anathema.

Ware felt that the concept of equality of sacrifice, that was current amongst the armed forces at the time, would have been swiftly eroded if there were to be any differentiation in memorial.[41] All had died in the service of their country he knew, and he thought that their death should be honoured in the same way.

---

[39] p.347. Brown.

[40] p.69, Jalland.

[41] P.314, Lewis-Stempel

> **LETTER FROM MR RUDYARD KIPLING.**
>
> TO THE EDITOR OF THE 'DAILY MAIL.'
>
> SIR,—A number of people from all parts of the world are visiting, and there is every sign that an immense number may be expected next year to visit, the French and Flanders Fronts and the Cemeteries behind. A portion of these visitors will be relatives or next-of-kin to the dead whose pilgrimages will be made with heavy hearts, but very many others will be drawn by curiosity and a natural interest in historical ground.
>
> But that ground, it should be remembered, is also holy—consecrated in every part by the freely-offered lives of men, and for that reason not to be overrun with levity.
>
> It is inevitable that the handling of such multitudes of sight seers must be managed on ordinary tourist lines; so it rests with the individual tourist to have respect for the spirit that lies upon all that land of desolation, and to walk through it with reverence.
>
> It is said that there is a tendency among some visitors to forget this obligation. Nothing would be gained by giving specific instances of what, after all, is more in the nature of unthinking carelessness than any intentional disrespect; but the Imperial War Graves Commission have asked me to express our most earnest hope that all who visit the battle areas will bear in mind that, at every step, they are in the presence of those dead through the merits of whose sacrifice they enjoy their present life, and whatever measure of freedom is theirs to-day.—I am, Sir, etc.,
>
> RUDYARD KIPLING.
>
> December 3rd, 1919.

Fig.12. Hull Daily Mail, 3rd December 1919.

In a statement the IGWC issued, in January 1918, the position was set out,

> 'The commission feels that it would be inadvisable to leave provision of memorials to private initiative. If memorials were allowed to be erected in the war cemeteries according to preference, taste and means of relatives and friends, the result would be that costly monuments put up by the well-to-do over their dead would contrast unkindly with those humbler ones which would be all that poorer folk could afford.'[42]

---

[42] p.33. Longworth.

The backlash against this idea has already been touched upon and the opposition used the same arguments as the exhumation issue. The main theme was that the family's personal choice should be sacrosanct, and that equality as a principle, rode roughshod over the family's feelings.

However, once again, the IGWC stood firm, bolstered by a letter that the Prince of Wales had sent them in 1917, in which he had said he had confidence in the Commission who,

> 'Will act about its task with the single aim of ensuring that the resting places of our soldiers and sailors shall always be reverently cared for and marked with permanent memorials worthy of the great cause for which they gave their lives.'[43]

The battle for the uniform headstone, or the principle of equality of sacrifice, was one thing and that particular battle raged on for some time.[44] The actual design of the stone, and what should be on it was another battle waged mainly internally between artists.

Suffice to say that the stone's dimensions were finally agreed to be 33 inches from its base and 15 inches broad and 3 inches wide and placed in a concrete base, after 1946 this base was known as a beam.[45] The design stipulated that it would be made from Portland Stone or Scottish Granite and be gently curved at the top to stop it weathering as much as possible. The lettering itself was designed by McDonald Gill, and it was so designed at a 45-degree angle to allow people to read it without having to bend down. A nod, perhaps to the fact, that it would no doubt be parents visiting the grave rather than younger people.[46]

Of course, alternatives were suggested and rejected. One of the most persistent ideas was that the stone should be in the shape of a cross. Ware was almost

---

[43] Hull Daily Mail, 24th November 1917.

[44] Sad to say this 'equality' extended only to the graves on the Western Front and European theatres of war. Olusaga writes, 'It was in 1922 that the British governor of what was then known as Tanganyika Territory – formerly German East Africa – wrote to officials at the IWGC, stating his opinion that it was 'a waste of Public money' to remember the dead of the Carrier Corps with individual graves.' P.420. Olusaga. This view appeared to be the predominant one in British Africa and mass graves were the norm for the Africans who lost their lives fighting for King and Country.

[45] p.43. Longworth.

[46] P.29. Summers.

desperate to avoid any religious symbolism being incorporated into the IWGC's work. It was noted, sometimes unfavourably in the press of the period, that there were no religious members on the Commission guiding panel. Ware felt that religious symbolism could not be used to embrace all the fallen as many of them were from different religions, especially in terms of the Empire forces that had died on the Western Front. He also knew that many of the soldiers of the Great War had seen, and suffered so much, in that intense period of their lives that any religious ideas of fighting a righteous war, with God on their side, had been destroyed in the mud and blood of the trenches.

However other people were not too sure about this stance. Arthur Balfour, the British Foreign Secretary, second only to the Prime Minister, David Lloyd George, had lost a son in the war and offered to design a suitable headstone in the form of a cross which he put forward for attention.[47] It was not a successful intervention and the original design was accepted. The decision was reported in the local press.

The fight for both simplicity and equality in the shape of the headstone had been won and, perhaps more surprisingly, the more controversial issue of what was written on them, was also resolved. As the illustration above makes clear, the name, regimental badge and a short inscription from the relatives were envisaged as the inscription on the stone.

The idea of incorporating the regimental badge was, in part, to alleviate the uniform dullness that it was felt that such cemeteries would present to the onlooker. National symbols from the Dominions and the Empire would all figure too. The name of the buried soldier or sailor, the rank, the regiment, date of death would also be included.

---

[47]That the design was not viewed favourably is probably an understatement. P.48, Longworth. Also, Ware was petitioned in the Spring of 1920 by at least 8,000 people who wanted a cross instead of the headstone design chosen and, as Crane writes, 'All Ware could see, or was prepared to see, were the same old Cecil names that figured in every protest.' Pp.148-149, Crane.

> **WAR HEROES' GRAVES.**
>
> Uniformity and simplicity are to distinguish the war cemeteries all over the world in which the British dead are buried. Every grave is to be marked by a headstone carrying the man's name, his regimental badge, and a short inscription chosen by his relatives. There has been some expression of sentiment that relatives should, if they so desired, choose individual memorials, but Mr Rudyard Kipling at a conference this afternoon, at which the Imperial War Graves Commission explained the scope of its work, emphasised the fact that the general desire was for equality, and that the treatment to be awarded to each grave should be uniform. Mr Winston Churchill, in elab…

Fig.13. Hull Daily Mail, 28th April 1920.

The personal inscription was to be a maximum of 60 characters and initially it was proposed that there was to be a charge made for each letter. Eventually, however, no charge was ever levied. The nature of the inscriptions was, of course, censored as,

> 'It is clearly undesirable to allow free scope for the effusions of the mortuary mason, the sentimental versifier, or the crank.'[48]

If IWGC thought that this gesture of magnanimity to the grieving families would earn them some respect from the disgruntled, who could neither choose a headstone or bring their child home, they were probably asking too much. Ruth Jervis, who lost her son in 1917, railed against the constriction of the length of inscription. In one letter to the IGWC she questioned,

> 'What next? May I ask how long we may remain at the graveside when we get there?'[49]

However, most people took up this opportunity and some inscriptions are quite moving perhaps due to their sparseness.

> 'At the foot of the grave is the inscription, paid for by the family: School, War, Death.'[50]

Some families however, reacted with more stoicism to their personal tragedies, and, in their fortitude did what the British working class have done since their creation and 'made the best of it.' Peter Lowden's great grandfather, William Gawthorpe, had seen two of his sons walk away to join the Army. One came back.

William's eldest son, Walter, was born in 1891, and had followed his father into the same industry, oil milling, which employed a large number of men and women in the area. The family had lived in the Wincolmlee part of the city for over half a century by the time of the Great War, and would continue to live in that area for another half a century after the Great War had ended. Walter had married Margaret McKinley in 1913. When the war was declared he enlisted in the 4th Battalion of the East Yorkshire Regiment on the 26th May 1915.

---

[48] p.34, Longworth.

[49] p.254, Van Emden, The Quick and the Dead. She goes on to say, 'I think we've come to a pretty state of things when a mother has to beg for the remains of her own boy. I want my boy home and I shall be satisfied with nothing less, and who has the right to deny me more under heaven.' The IWGC did not continue this correspondence.

[50] P.308, Van Emden, Boy Soldiers.

Fig.14. Walter Gawthorpe, probably on his wedding day, Christmas Day 1913. Aged 22.

Walter was transferred to the Western Front at the end of 1915 and he fought at the battles of the Somme, Passchendaele, and Oppy Wood. He was wounded in January 1916 after only a few months at the front. The wound was not serious and he returned to the front later that year in time for the Somme offensive.

Walter's regiment had been so badly mauled at the Oppy Wood fight that the regiment was left with only a cadre of men and so was amalgamated into the 1st Battalion of the 8th Lancashire Fusiliers.

After weathering the Kaiser's Offensive, the last gasp of the German forces in the March and April of 1918, he was involved in the battle of Amiens, which was the beginning of the Allied forces' pushing back the German forces which only ended on the Rhine and the Armistice.

On the 14th of August 1918, he and his platoon sergeant, were scouting ahead of the advance troops when they were both hit by rifle fire. Sergeant. Batty was killed outright. Walter's body was recovered but he died in a front-line dressing station.

Walter was buried in Bertrancourt cemetery. This cemetery had been established in 1916 for battlefield burials and it is approximately 16 kilometres from Albert, scene of heavy fighting throughout the war.

Walter's father, William, although 48 years old at the time, also enlisted in June 1915, but was obviously unsuited for active service, so was transferred to the Royal Defence Corps. This was the Great War's equivalent of the Home Guard of the Second World War although a much more professional outfit.

We can only guess at what effect the news of the death of their eldest son had upon the parents, what we do know is that William was posted to France in June 1919. Whether this was of his own volition by volunteering or some other reason we will never know We do know that William went to France and assisted in the Labour Corps, exhuming bodies and burying them in the IWGC cemeteries that were springing up and one day he managed to visit his boy's grave, the moment captured in Fig.16.

Fig.15. Walter at the front. Gone is the happy smile and those eyes have seen more than we can barely imagine.

Fig.16. William, stood proudly, with his hand upon the wooden cross marking his son's grave.

Fig.17. Bertrancourt Cemetery, 2017.

Fig.18. Walter's headstone, 2017.

Of course, William wasn't the only member of the family who wanted to visit Walter's grave. In 1922 the family had scraped enough money to allow two members to visit. Pete's grandmother wasn't a member of the select party as she was pregnant with Tom, his future uncle.[51]

Fig.19. The family visit to Walter's grave.

---

[51] Because the photograph in Fig 19 is so old and degraded with age, and of course, our generation weren't present at the visit, nor is there any writing on the back, we, who are left, disagree pleasantly about who is pictured in this photograph. I'm now inclined to believe that on the right is Walter's mother and to the left of the photograph is his wife, Margaret. Of course, it's only my guess.

Walter wasn't the only member of an author's family to lose someone in the Great War. Michael Kelly, the cemetery superintendent, is a direct ancestor of Bill's wife, Jeanne. Michael's son, also called Michael, fell in 1916 and was buried in France in a war time cemetery.

Fig.20. Michael Kelly's grave before the erection of the IGWC headstone.

Many families erected shrines within their houses, as well as the communities erecting more public street shrines. Below is a photograph of Pete's grandmother sitting below a photograph collage. In the second left section at the top of the wall plaque is a photograph of Walter, her brother.

Fig. 21. Jenny Lowden, nee Gawthorpe, with the shrine behind her.

Fig.22. The Street Shrine in Grange Street. Pete was born in that street in the early 1950's and said that the shrine had long disappeared by that time.

More public shows of grief have been touched upon, as in the setting up of street shrines to honour the men who had died. In Hull approximately 70,000 men served in the armed forces, and of that total at least 9,000 were killed as well as a considerable amount of wounded.[52] As such, along with large and small

---

[52] p.137. O'Neill.

communities throughout the land, Hull wanted its civic war memorial. The French offered their communities a small subsidy towards the cost of erecting them, but the British usually relied upon donations from the public or industry.

As we have seen, the large Cenotaph in Whitehall, was often taken as a model for the memorial, as it did not have any religious connotations, and could symbolise many things to many people. Before the Cenotaph in Hull was erected however, the Armistice was scrupulously observed.[53] In an article in the Hull Daily Mail, headed by the headline, **Hull Remembers the Great Deliverance**, it described how the 'great silence' was observed in the city. The part referring to Paragon Station gives the flavour,

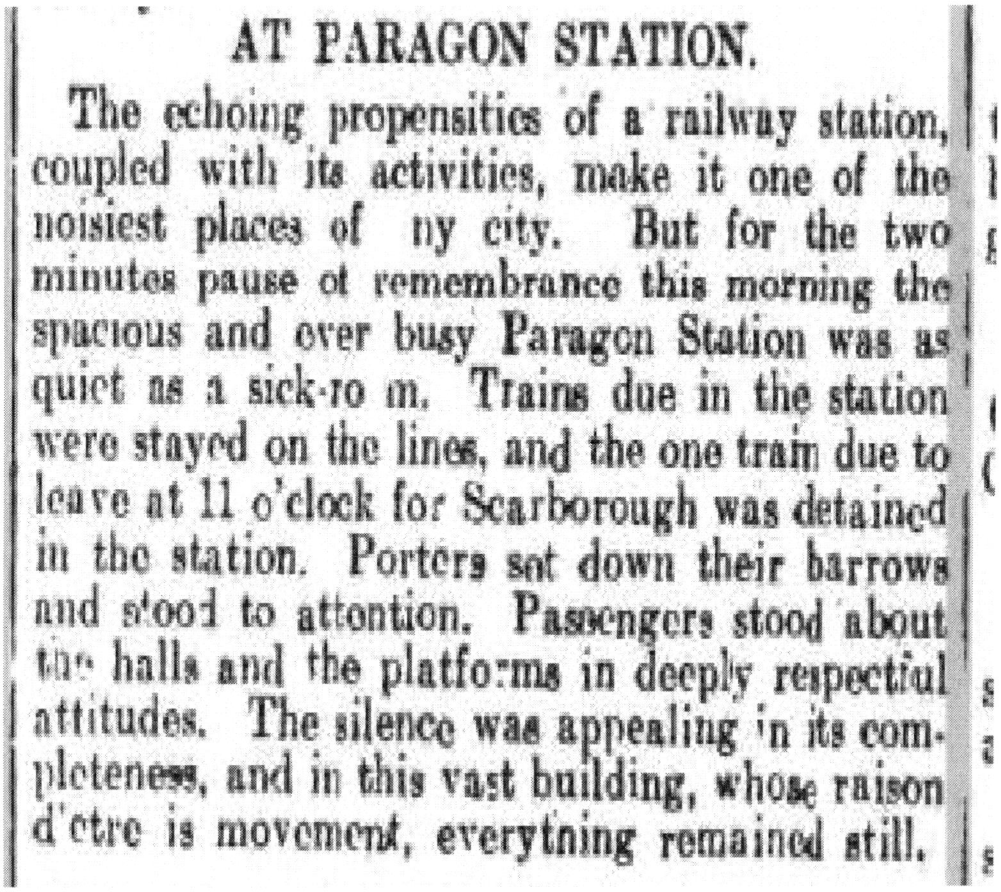

> **AT PARAGON STATION.**
>
> The echoing propensities of a railway station, coupled with its activities, make it one of the noisiest places of ny city. But for the two minutes pause of remembrance this morning the spacious and ever busy Paragon Station was as quiet as a sick-room. Trains due in the station were stayed on the lines, and the one train due to leave at 11 o'clock for Scarborough was detained in the station. Porters set down their barrows and stood to attention. Passengers stood about the halls and the platforms in deeply respectful attitudes. The silence was appealing in its completeness, and in this vast building, whose raison d'etre is movement, everything remained still.

Fig.23. Hull Daily Mail. 11th November 1919.

---

[53] P.549, Stevenson.

In 1921, the newspaper once again gave great prominence to the Armistice observation, under the headline, **The Silent City,** and it dominated the entire front page. Coupled with this was the beginning of the annual poppy sale in aid the General, later Earl, Haig fund to support the disabled ex-service personnel of the conflict.

> **SALE OF POPPIES.**
>
> **EX-LADY MAYORESS'S SUPPLY EXHAUSTED.**
>
> The ex-Lady Mayoress (Mrs T. Beecroft Atkinson) desires to inform the public that owing to the Headquarters, British Legion, having only forwarded half the quantity of Flanders Poppies ordered by her, she regrets that all her supplies became exhausted early this morning owing to the enormous demand for them, and wishes to apologise to those who were unable to purchase poppies.
>
> The ex-Lady Mayoress wishes to express her deep gratitude to her numerous helpers throughout the City, who rallied splendidly to help forward the cause for which these poppies were sold.

Fig.24. Hull Daily Mail, 11th November 1921.

By 1923, the phenomenon showed no sign of abatement. Indeed, with the possibility of the city's own cenotaph now on the horizon, it appeared to gather steam.

HULL CITIZENS' MAGNIFICENT TRIBUTE TO THOSE WHO SERVED SO FAITHFULLY.

A SORROW IN WHICH PRIDE HAS A PART.

PEN PICTURES OF SUNDAY'S PROCESSION AND CENOTAPH WREATH LAYING.

£1,200 FOR EARL HAIG'S FUND.

Fig.25. Hull Daily Mail, 9th November 1923.

Of course, Hull did have much of which to be proud and sad.

WHAT CENOTAPH STANDS FOR

TWELVE THOUSAND HULL MEN WHO DID NOT COME BACK.

CITY'S PERMANENT MEMORIAL

The Hull Cenotaph will be ready for unveiling in the early part of next Spring.

As described in the "Mail" the foundation stone was laid on Thursday afternoon.

The architect for the Cenotaph is Mr T. Harold Hughes, A.R.I.B.A., of Glasgow, who states it will be a simple mass, and in keeping with the simplicity of the South African memorial, which is to be lowered and incorporated in the lay-out. Wing wall will extend from the Cenotaph to the ends of the eastern boundary of the site. In the centre of the area is to be a plot of grass surrounded by steps, which will link together the Cenotaph and the South African Memorial. The contractors are Quibell and Son, Ltd., Hull.

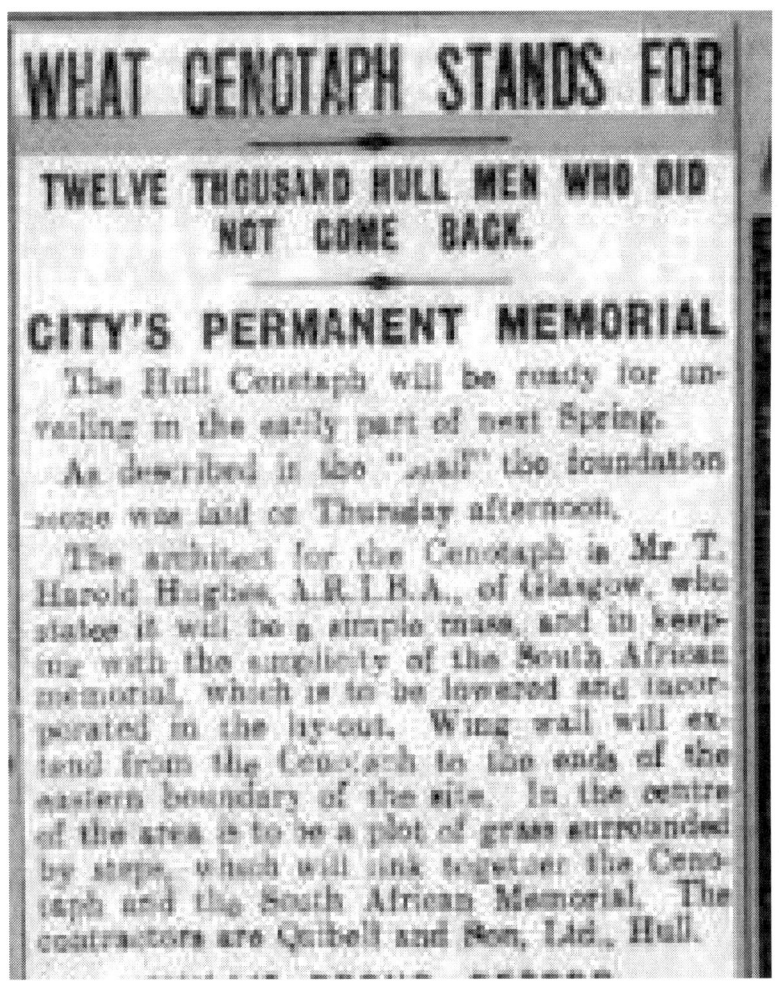

Fig.26. Hull Daily Mail, 9th November 1923.

1924 gave the public their first views of what was to become the Hull Cenotaph or War Memorial. Other sites for it had been investigated, such as next to the proposed Hull Ferens Art Gallery, but all had failed to be accepted in one way or another. At one point, the proposal was that the memorial to the soldiers of the South African War was to be moved, and placed in the front of the Royal Station Hotel, but the LNER objected saying it needed the land.

A compromise was reached in that the South African Memorial was to be reduced in height and the new memorial placed to the east of it. As the image above states, Quibell, the builder, bid for the project and won the contract in October 1923. Probably a bitter-sweet moment, for George Quibell, the owner's son, had been killed in the conflict. The artist's depiction of the site had been aired in the Hull Daily Mail a month earlier than this announcement.

Fig.27. Hull Daily Mail, 23rd September 1923.

In the November another sketch simply whetted the appetite of the public. This outlined the route of the procession that was to parade past the site of the new memorial.

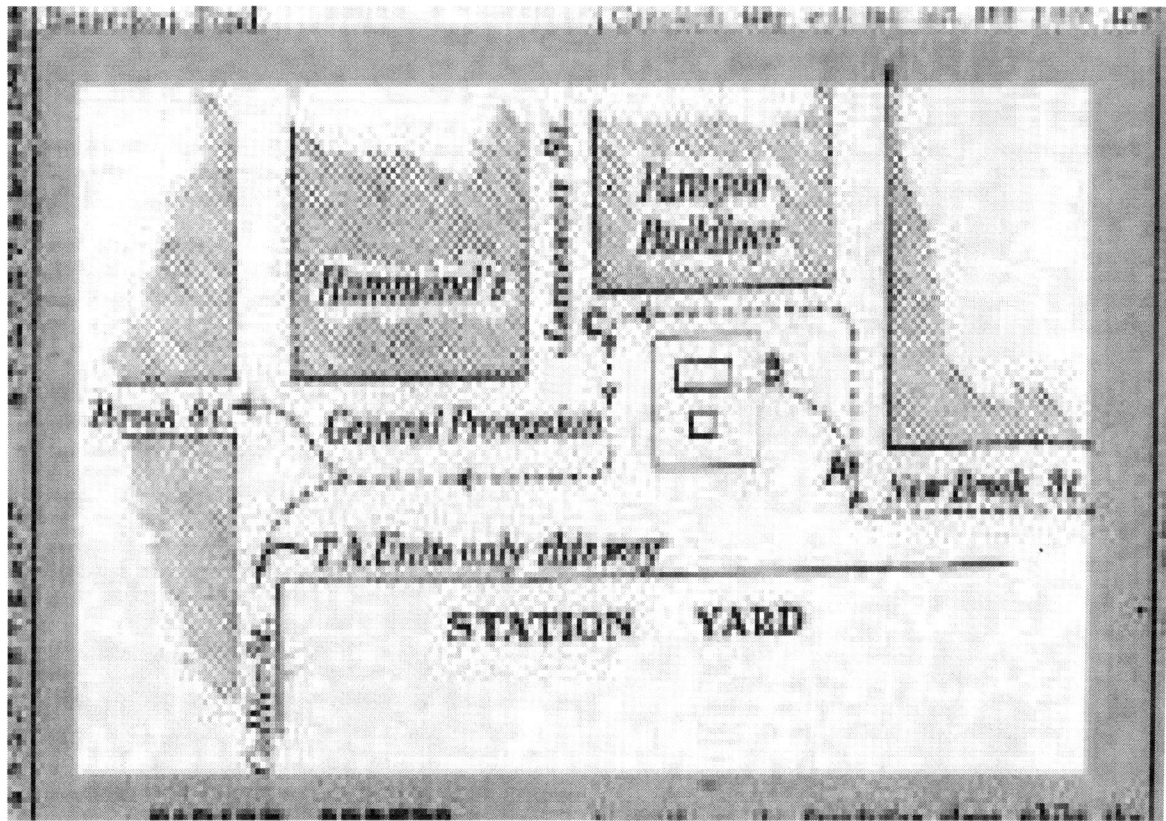

Fig.28. Hull Daily Mail, 23rd November 1923.

By the June of 1924 the memorial began to take form and the Hull Daily Mail showed the progress.

All of this build up to the official opening was almost guaranteed to make an emotional outpouring of grief even more of a certainty. The newspaper was full of the impending ceremony for the official opening, weeks before the actual date. HRH Prince Albert, the future King George VI, was announced to be officially unveiling it, although this role fell to Field Marshall Robertson on the day.

The BBC broadcast the ceremony live on the new national wireless service. Even better, in the age of the local cinema's heyday, The Strand, on Beverley Road, advertised that they had captured the entire unveiling ceremony, and would be showing it to the public.

Fig.29. Hull Daily Mail, 30th June 1924.

"Pals." The management of the Strand has always maintained its reputation for enterprise, and Mr Cartledge has filmed an exclusive picture of the unveiling of Hull's Cenotaph, which will be screened from Wednesday next. The feature film for the latter part of the week will be "The Blindness of Richard."

Fig.30. Hull Daily Mail, 24th September 1924.

With the recording and filming of the memorial service, an argument could now begin to be made that what had been a ceremony of remembrance had become entertainment. It could now be listened to without the discomfort of leaving your cosy armchair, and if you wanted, you could take your girl or boy friend to the local cinema to see if you could pick out any of your friends at the ceremony.

Fig.31. Hull Daily Mail, 22nd September 1924.

Fig.32. The unveiling of the Hull Cenotaph.

In Hull this unveiling ceremony appears to have been the culmination of the public show of grief that the Great War demanded of the survivors. Attendance at subsequent Armistice Days began to fall off, especially in the 1930's, when the rise of Fascism provoked thoughts that the sacrifice of the sons and daughters of Hull in the 'War to End All Wars' may well have all been in vain. The ceremonies themselves also began to take on some religious aspects of which the originators of the ceremony would never have meant it be invested. This falling off, to some extent, of the meaning of the ceremony to many, was not confined to Hull. However, a letter from Bill's grandmother perhaps shows how the Remembrance Day ceremony in Hull was beginning to be treated.

ARMISTICE DAY.

TO THE EDITOR.

Sir,—Would you kindly allow me a small space in your valuable paper, as I would like what I have to say to meet the eyes of certain "young ladies" near the Cenotaph.

Their conduct was a disgrace to the citizens of Hull, who were gathered round the cenotaph for the purpose of hearing the service, and to bring their offerings for the departed brave. All one could hear was their outbursts of laughter and remarks, above the preacher's voice.

I think in the future that those who are devoid of common sense should be kept in the background on such an occasion, as it wounds the feelings of those who witness such gross ignorance.—I am, Sir, etc.,

MARY E. LONGBONE.
16, Leonards-avenue, Courtney-street,
Hull, November 12th, 1925.

Fig.33. Bill's grandmother's letter to the Hull Daily Mail.

Fig.34. The Cenotaph and Paragon Square in the 1930's.

Of course, the private grief of the survivors still continued.[54] The public shrines, the marching bands, the laying of wreaths at public ceremonies may have been fashionable, but the desire to visit the grave of the loved one, or if not that, the spot where they died, was a desire that could not be assuaged by the pomp and ritual demanded by public ceremony. In private communion with the grave, the grieving relative could allow emotion, be it sorrow, anger or simply resignation, to be expressed openly without the conduit of ritual. The war grave was that place to lose oneself in grief, knowing that others who would be there, would have a shared knowledge, an affinity with you if you sobbed, cried, or even howled and cursed in your grief.

By this time the IWGC had been created by an Order in Council in May 1917 after long debate and argument. Ware felt that the organization that should care for the war dead should be 'Imperial' in outlook. By this he meant it should be a shared responsibility of the countries that were involved in the fighting, rather than it become simply another government department of the mother country. He believed that if it did not do this, it would be subject to Treasury rules and, in time, the care of the cemeteries would suffer.

He managed to convince influential people of the soundness of his ideas on this, including Churchill and the Prince of Wales. He also managed to recruit the representatives of the Dominions and other colonies of the time to his side. The treasury was unhappy with the arrangement, but once a formula was devised where the cost of the upkeep of the cemeteries was to be shared on the basis of the proportion of the war dead within the cemeteries, the funding for the cemeteries was assured. This arrangement is still in force today.

Concurrently, the work that had been undertaken in both France and Belgium and, of course, the other places around the world where Britain's war dead had fallen, and were buried other tasks needed attention. The IWGC also took in hand the burials of the war dead in the home countries. As the IWGC replied to the Town Clerk of Hull,

---

[54] Violet Cecil, quoted in Jalland, placed an In Memoriam in **The Times** for the first time in 1934 for her son George, killed in 1914. She later noted in her diary of that day, 'It is twenty years ago since he was killed. The sorrow, the loss, the pain, are as great today as in 1914.' In 1945 she confided to someone who had lost their son in WW2, 'And I have not yet recovered. You will not recover. One grows a carapace. That is all.' P.55-56, Jalland.

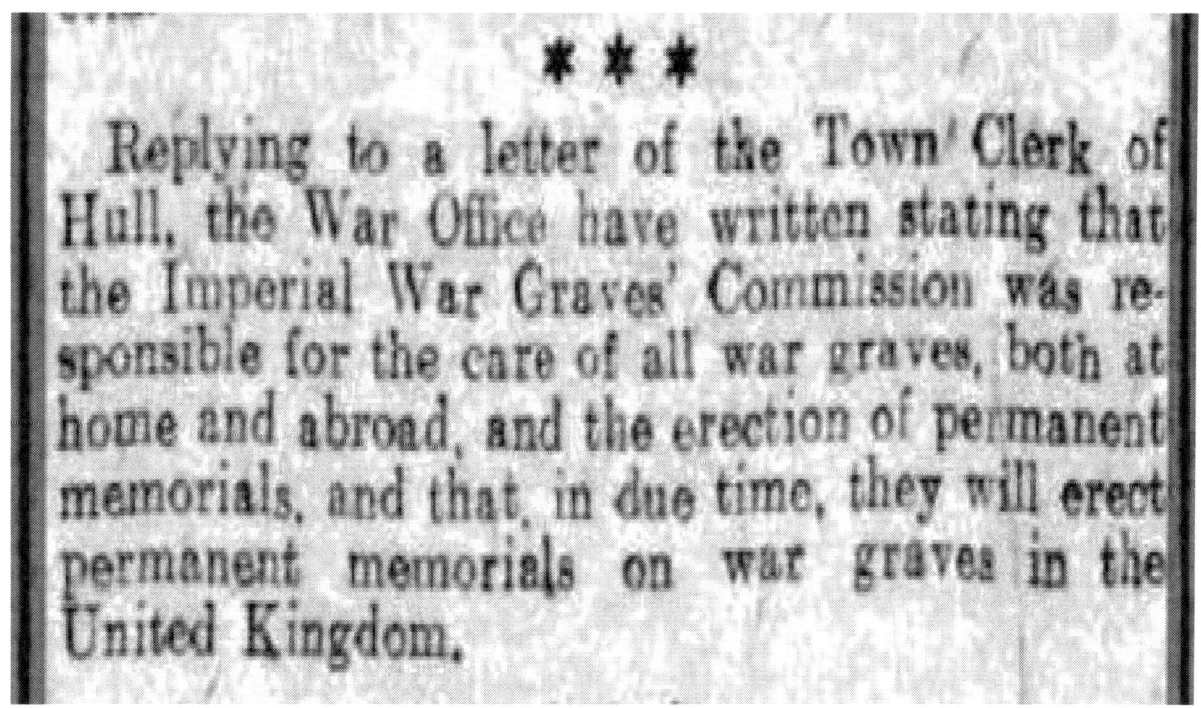

Fig.35. Hull Daily Mail, 1st March 1921.

The provision of providing war graves, to the design used in the war cemeteries on the continent, was to follow the same rules as had been accepted earlier. Obviously, the concept of non-exhumation did not apply here. The headstone would be erected upon the grave plot, usually the family plot, if the family desired it. If they already had a headstone then they could have another one erected at the foot of the grave, following the model used in Europe. In this way, sometimes graves appeared to have two 'heads' with a headstone at both ends.

The design on the headstone also followed the principles as laid down in the cemeteries in Europe. If the family did not have a headstone, the IWGC would provide their standard one, but only to record the details of the lost soldier or sailor. By April of the next year the IWGC had been in contact with the necessary authority in Hull,

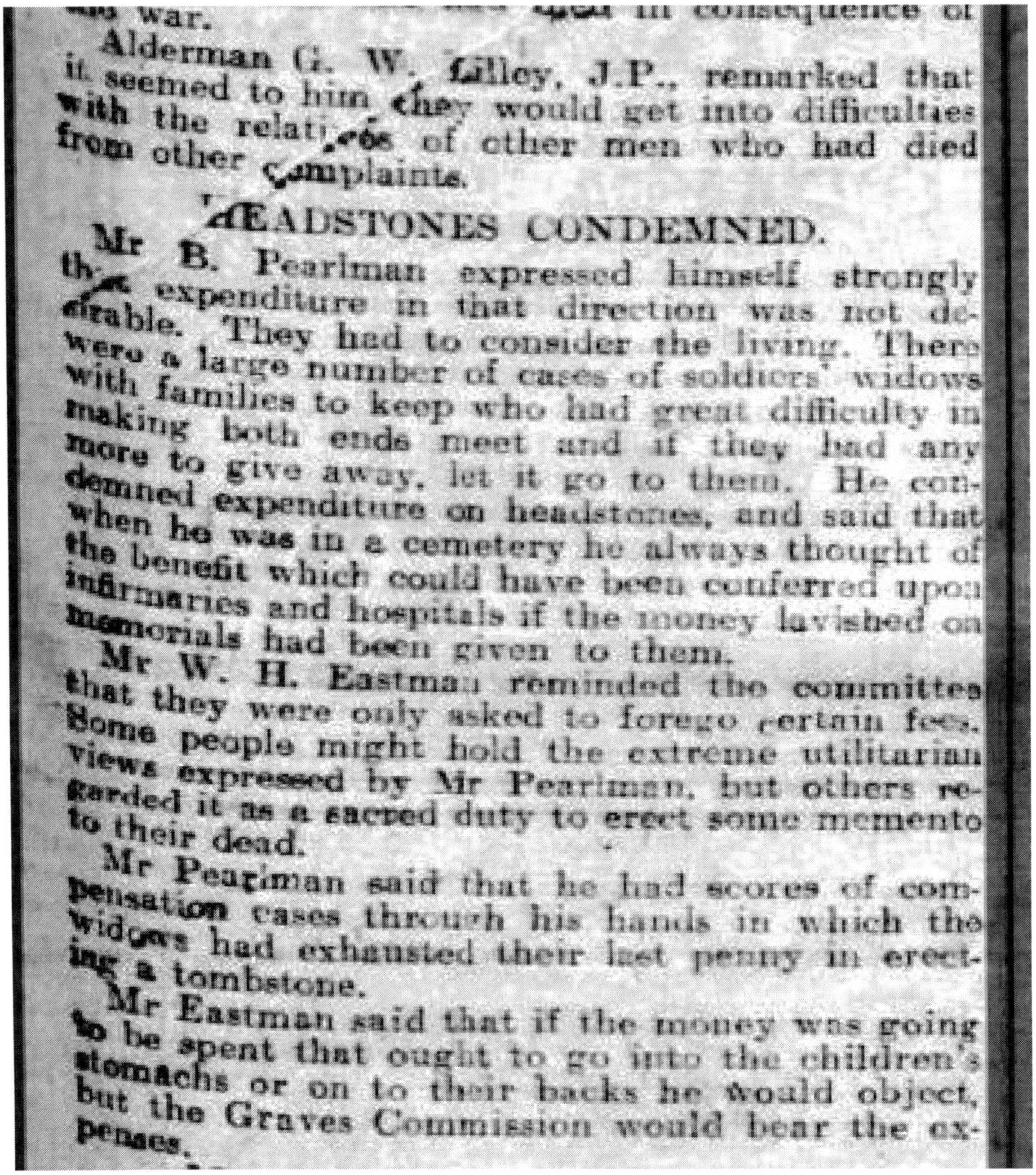

> ...war.
>
> Alderman G. W. Lilley, J.P., remarked that it seemed to him they would get into difficulties with the relatives of other men who had died from other complaints.
>
> **HEADSTONES CONDEMNED.**
>
> Mr B. Pearlman expressed himself strongly that expenditure in that direction was not desirable. They had to consider the living. There were a large number of cases of soldiers' widows with families to keep who had great difficulty in making both ends meet and if they had any more to give away, let it go to them. He condemned expenditure on headstones, and said that when he was in a cemetery he always thought of the benefit which could have been conferred upon infirmaries and hospitals if the money lavished on memorials had been given to them.
>
> Mr W. H. Eastman reminded the committee that they were only asked to forego certain fees. Some people might hold the extreme utilitarian views expressed by Mr Pearlman, but others regarded it as a sacred duty to erect some memento to their dead.
>
> Mr Pearlman said that he had scores of compensation cases through his hands in which the widows had exhausted their last penny in erecting a tombstone.
>
> Mr Eastman said that if the money was going to be spent that ought to go into the children's stomachs or on to their backs he would object, but the Graves Commission would bear the expenses.

Fig.36. Hull Daily Mail, 13th April 1922.

Surprisingly, this request caused some consternation in the council chamber. Mr Benno Pearlman objected strongly to this request. He said that he condemned expenditure on headstones and whenever he was in a cemetery,

> 'He always thought of the benefit which could be conferred upon infirmaries and hospitals if the money lavished on memorials had been given to them.'[55]

---

[55] Hull Daily Mail, 13th April 1922.

When one sees that the IWGC were only requesting that the fees for erecting the stones in the local cemeteries were waived, this seems to be a churlish attack, and it was pointed out that his 'extreme utilitarian views' did not chime with others. The Corporation approved the suggestion made by the IWGC and the fees were waived.

By October 1922 plans had begun to take shape in Hull,

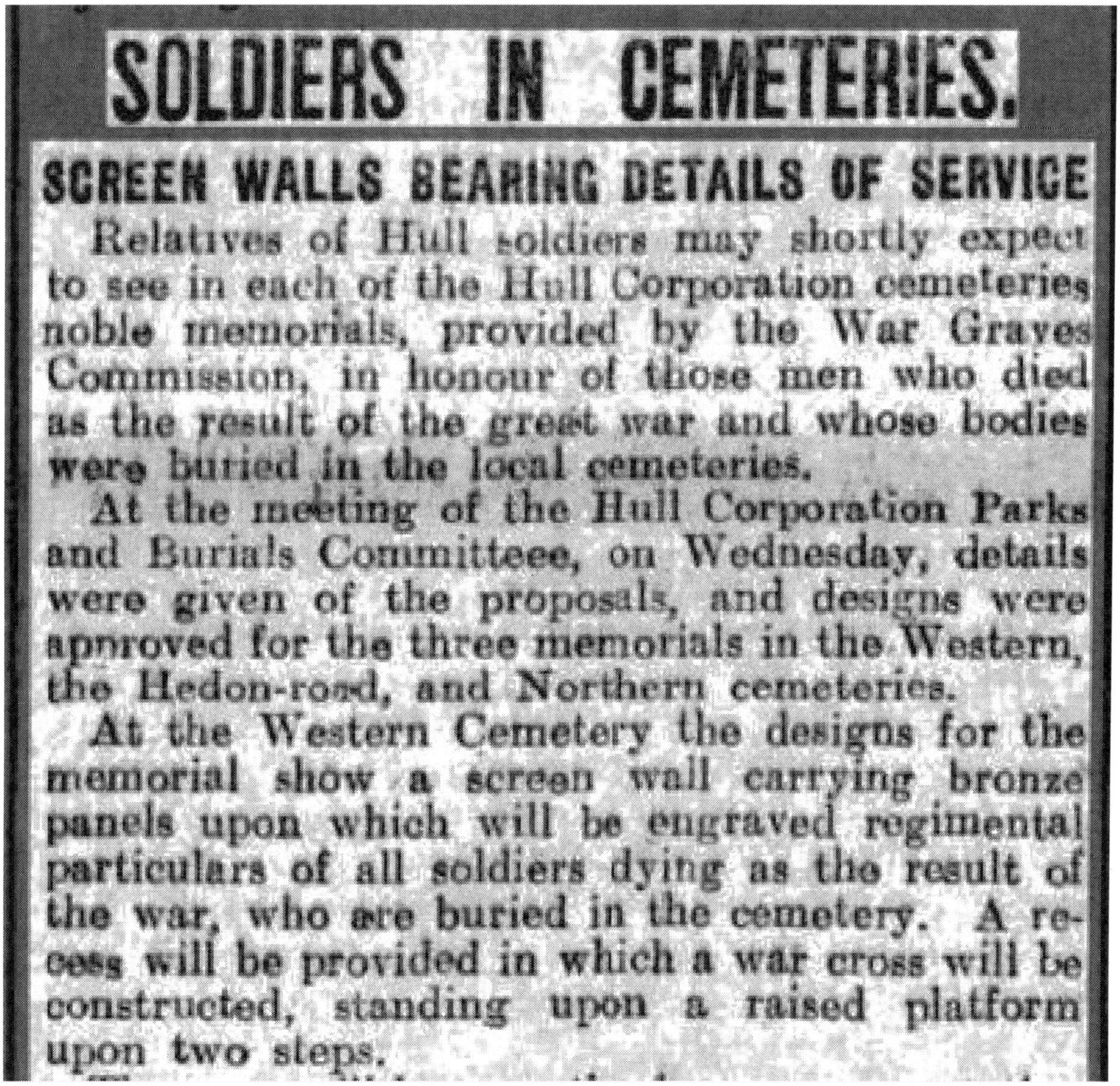

SOLDIERS IN CEMETERIES.
SCREEN WALLS BEARING DETAILS OF SERVICE

Relatives of Hull soldiers may shortly expect to see in each of the Hull Corporation cemeteries noble memorials, provided by the War Graves Commission, in honour of those men who died as the result of the great war and whose bodies were buried in the local cemeteries.

At the meeting of the Hull Corporation Parks and Burials Committees, on Wednesday, details were given of the proposals, and designs were approved for the three memorials in the Western, the Hedon-road, and Northern cemeteries.

At the Western Cemetery the designs for the memorial show a screen wall carrying bronze panels upon which will be engraved regimental particulars of all soldiers dying as the result of the war, who are buried in the cemetery. A recess will be provided in which a war cross will be constructed, standing upon a raised platform upon two steps.

Fig.37. Hull Daily Mail, 12th October 1922.

As may be seen, developments had progressed and, like all the cemeteries where more than 40 war dead were laid to rest, a Cross of Sacrifice was planned to be erected in Western Cemetery. The article goes on to say,

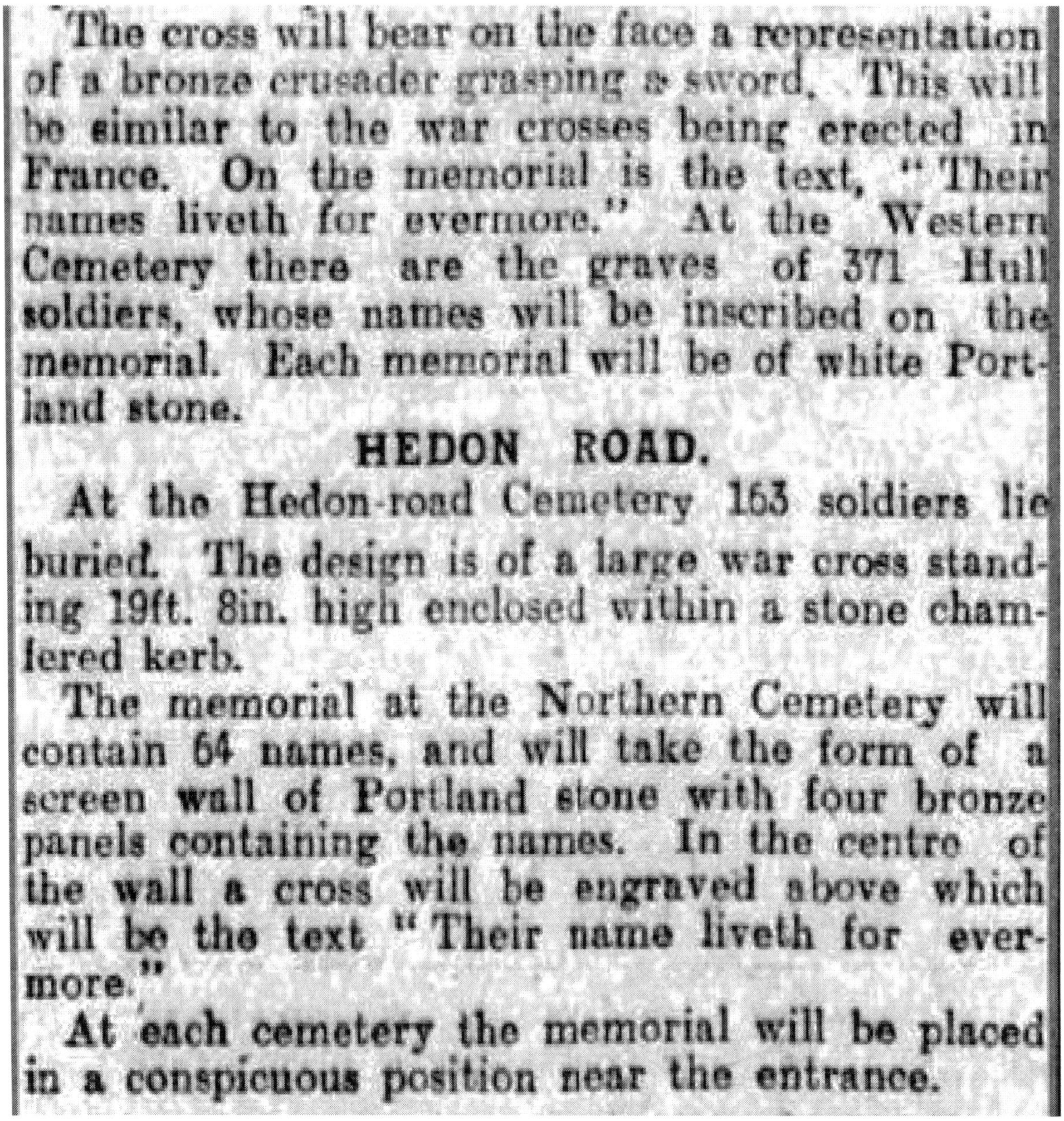

> The cross will bear on the face a representation of a bronze crusader grasping a sword. This will be similar to the war crosses being erected in France. On the memorial is the text, "Their names liveth for evermore." At the Western Cemetery there are the graves of 371 Hull soldiers, whose names will be inscribed on the memorial. Each memorial will be of white Portland stone.
>
> **HEDON ROAD.**
>
> At the Hedon-road Cemetery 163 soldiers lie buried. The design is of a large war cross standing 19ft. 8in. high enclosed within a stone chamfered kerb.
>
> The memorial at the Northern Cemetery will contain 64 names, and will take the form of a screen wall of Portland stone with four bronze panels containing the names. In the centre of the wall a cross will be engraved above which will be the text "Their name liveth for evermore."
>
> At each cemetery the memorial will be placed in a conspicuous position near the entrance.

Fig.38. Hull Daily Mail, 12th October 1922.

With this project in hand the Hull municipal cemeteries acquired the accoutrements that graced the war cemeteries in Europe. The Cross of Sacrifice was overtly religious in its design and was Fabian Ware's sole concession in this direction. He was not alone in this view.[56] The designer of this structure, Reginald Blomfield, allowed his design to be reduced to accommodate the structure in smaller cemeteries.[57]

---

[56] P.471. Laqueur. 'Keep the poisonous sculptures out of the plan'. After the Great War this view was common against the established religions.

[57] P.28, Summers shows a very good illustration of this process.

The Stone of Remembrance, designed by Sir Edwin Lutyens, who also designed the Cenotaph in Whitehall, was deliberately designed with no overt religious significance, although Lutyens believed that people may take the structure as some form of altar, if they so desired. The Stone was designed to be placed in cemeteries with over 400 war dead in them.

Hull General Cemetery also had some of the war dead buried within its ground. Unfortunately, the information regarding the interaction between Hull General Cemetery and the IWGC is poor. The problem lies with the fact that the cemetery records are patchy because much of the paper work of the cemetery was sent for pulping during the Second World War, in response to the Government's paper drives.

Suffice to say that Hull General Cemetery was contacted in October 1917 enquiring of how many war burials had been conducted in the cemetery since the war had begun. (see Appendix 3) That this was a circular letter that must have been sent to the Borough too, in regard to their cemeteries, is evident from the wording.

The Superintendent of Hull General Cemetery, Michael Kelly, replied with a list of seven names, later adding three more taking the list up to March 1918. Eventually, at the end of the Great War, it had fourteen official war graves. This increased after the Second World War with another fourteen graves which gave an official war grave total of 28 burials. Unofficially there were considerably more.

The principle of 'permanence', that the governments of the then British Empire had, was a policy that, 'Collectively pledged the permanence of graves and memorials at the Imperial Conference in 1918. In the past, headstones and memorials that had any degree of permanence had been rare and reserved for a few exalted beings; the Commission was dealing with vast numbers of men, most of them private soldiers.'[58]

When that principle of permanence was or is threatened, and that could range from the stone itself deteriorating to cemeteries becoming derelict, it was and is beholden upon the IWGC (now the CWGC) to step in and correct the fault. In

---

[58] P.66, Gibson and Ward.

the 1970's Pete well remembers the CWGC attending quite regularly to attend to some deterioration in the Stone of Remembrance in Northern Cemetery.

Fig.39. The Cross of Sacrifice, Western Cemetery, Hull

This is a constant part of the organization's remit and it is fair to say that it takes a significant part of its budget.

In Hull General Cemetery's case the problem lay with its failure to keep the cemetery in a fit state. One of the terms that the IWGC (and CWGC) used/uses in cases like this is 'unmaintainable'. In 1960 the Cemetery was effectively warned that the CWGC felt the cemetery was becoming 'unmaintainable' and this was noted in the minute book of the Company for that year.[59] However, for the Cemetery Company, this was nowhere near the top of the issues that it faced at that time.

When the CGWC inspected once again, they saw that nothing had changed, indeed the CGWC probably thought that things had got worse and told the Cemetery Company that the stones would be removed. This was done in October 1965 when an affidavit was agreed between the Cemetery Company and the CGWC by Deed of Covenant to remove the 28 war grave headstones in the cemetery.

However, this was only the removal of the headstones not the exhumation of the bodies. As we've seen previously, exhumation of one of the war dead is something that is not undertaken lightly, and, although the CGWC thought the headstones may be at risk, and therefore invoked the policy with regard to 'permanence', they did not feel that the actual bodies were at risk.

Although the CGWC actually stipulated the number of headstones to be removed as 28, they in fact removed only 27 and it is difficult to understand why this happened, unless by simple omission or mistake. Obviously, the risk pertained to all of the headstones and not just 27 of them. Something of a mystery.

---

[59] 'Their purpose in doing this is to substitute them for small blocks in a wall of remembrance being built in the Northern Cemetery, and they want to get all the commemoration tablets in one place in Hull if this can be managed, mainly to save maintenance costs for which they are responsible. Agreed to allow Commission to remove the headstones.' 11th July 1960., Hull General Cemetery minute book. Of course, the Commission could have removed the stones anyway as they have the legal right imposed upon them to maintain the stones. The Company was once again deluding itself.

When headstones, such as the ones in Hull General Cemetery, are removed to another site, most usually a replica headstone or plaque is sited with the phrase,' Buried in so and so Cemetery'. This is what has happened in Northern Cemetery with regard to the Hull General Cemetery war dead.

This custom harks back to very beginning of the IWGC and has its roots in what Rudyard Kipling termed, 'dud graves'. As you may remember Kipling lost his son and there were no remains left of him. Therefore, the Kiplings had no grave to visit but, the Kiplings were not the only ones suffering like this. Kipling asked many of the people, in the same position as him and his wife, bereft of a place to go to grieve their loss, and the majority of the people suffering did not want to visit a false grave. They were quite prepared to have their loved one recorded on a memorial tablet or plaque, or in grander style on the War Memorials that were planned to be erected in Northern France at Thiepval and Ypres at that time.

Kipling took these views back to the Commission and strongly argued the case, especially against an Australian proposal that backed the idea of a headstone for every soldier or sailor whether they were buried there or not. In the end the Commission accepted the premise that in every war grave that had to be a body.

Fig.40. Northern Cemetery, Hull.

Kipling was also responsible for the wording on other memorials found in the war cemeteries. Kipling knew as well as anyone the pain of having a loved one being classed as 'missing', and this was a significant proportion of the war dead from the Great War. Having this insight, it was he who formulated the wording that would be inscribed on both the individual headstones of an unknown soldier or on the larger memorials and plaques that commemorated the dead, where no body had ever been recovered.

On the individual headstones of the unidentified, the wording was decided to include the phrase, 'A Soldier of the Great War' and 'Known unto God'. When no remains of the body could be buried, memorial plaques where it involved smaller numbers, up to the massive structures built in the inter war period which memorialised thousands of missing men, were inscribed with the following words that Kipling chose, 'Their Glory Shall Not Be Blotted Out', a phrase which he took from the Bible.

Some 100 years after the Great War finished, and almost 80 years after the Second World War began, the Armistice ceremony is still resonant with meaning and emotion. The long-serried lines of headstones in the war cemeteries in France and Belgium can cause you to catch your breath, not only at the amount, but also at the tranquil beauty of the scene. The echoes of the Last Post can still create goose bumps on the listener. We are all descendants of people who lived through those great conflicts of the twentieth century and we are all still touched by the repercussions of those conflicts today. How could we forget? Our past was their present; their present was fought for our future.

Section Two

There are 3 basic categories of servicemen's graves in Hull General Cemetery:

1. Men buried with no remaining headstone
2. Men buried that are inscribed on a family headstone
3. Men buried elsewhere, but recorded on a headstone

1.Servicemen buried in Hull General Cemetery, who are now listed on the Commemorative Plaque in Northern Cemetery

The remains of the following 28 men were all buried in Hull General Cemetery, and each was commemorated with a headstone or plaque, and recorded by the CWGC. As outlined in Section One, the CWGC, became concerned that the graves were 'unmaintainable,' and after discussions with the Hull General Cemetery Company, it was decided to remove the CWGC headstones, and record the men's names on a plaque in Hull's Northern Cemetery. This was undertaken and the headstones removed, although one CWGC headstone, (Private 10/166 John Hodgson) was left standing, as it was on a family grave, this is the only remaining CWGC headstone in the cemetery.

Two other headstones, although not IWGC ones, dedicated to Captain William Donaldson and Lieutenant Colonel Richard Ethelbert Johnson still remain. The headstone on the family grave where Captain George Shetliff Wood is buried, still remains, but there is no inscription dedicated to him.

1a. The Great War

Sergeant 3/7316 Herbert John Alexander of the 7th Battalion, East Yorkshire Regiment was born in Hull in 1876. He married Florence May Garside at the Hull Register Office in 1906, and had four children. Before the outbreak of the Great War, he had already served for several years in India and Somaliland, where he had received a medal and clasp. He was invalided out of the Army in December 1914. At the time of his death in 1916 the family were living in Wassand Street, a small street off Hessle Road.

Private 21619 William Henry Blackbourn of the 12th Battalion, East Yorkshire Regiment was born 1895 in Hull, the son of Mr. William Alison Blackbourn, a rope manufacturer, and Mrs Emily Blackburn (nee Hakes), who lived at 9 Fish St Hull. Prior to joining the Army, William was an Iron Fettler.

He suffered serious gunshot wounds to the back and abdomen, whilst fighting at Etaples in France on the 12th August 1916, and was returned to England for medical treatment. Unfortunately, he died of complications to his wounds, at the military hospital in Cambridge, with his mother present on 15th November 1916.

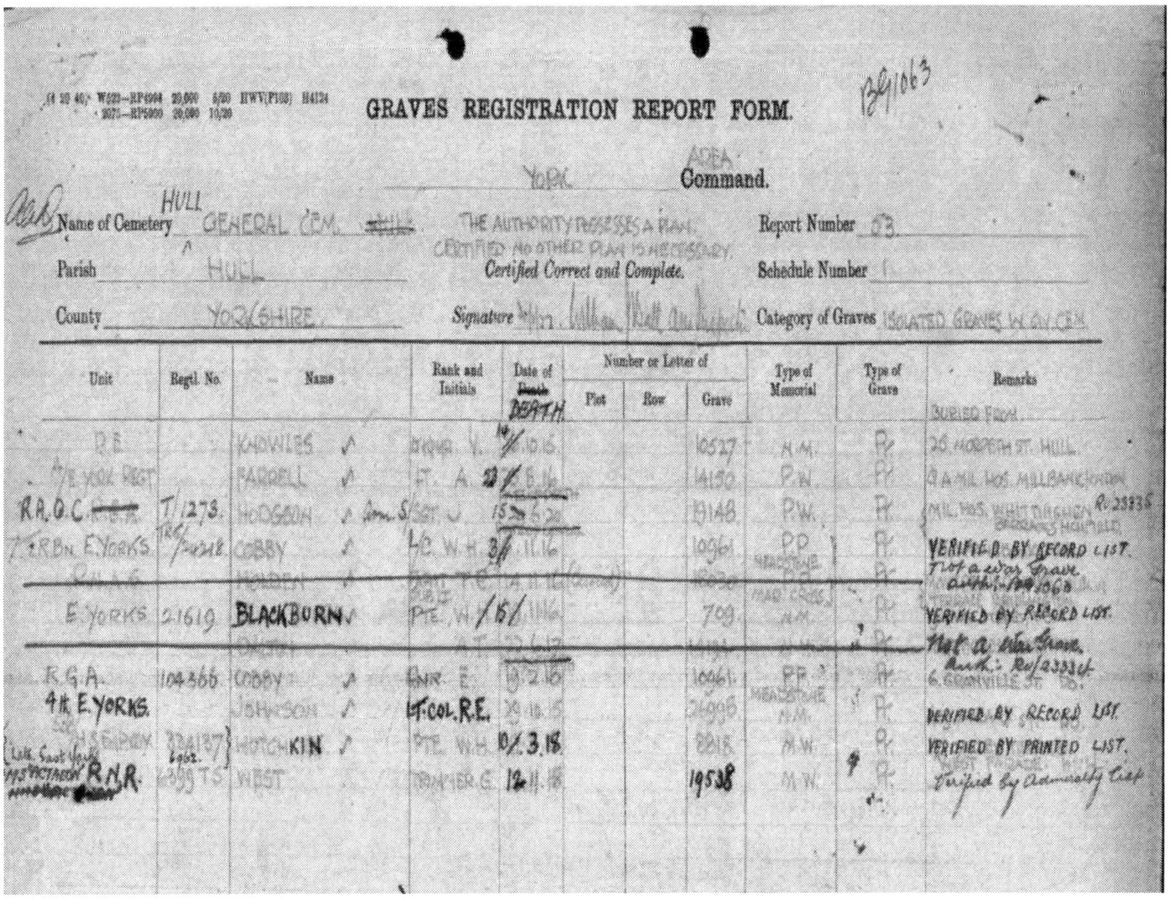

He was buried in Hull General Cemetery and is commemorated on the panel in Northern Cemetery. There is no memorial on his grave in Hull General Cemetery.

Fig.41. Private Blackbourn's grave listing for the IWGC, dated 1922.

Lance Corporal 24218 Walter Harold Cobby and Gunner 104366 Ernest Cobby were two brothers, who died in the Great War, and who are buried in Hull General Cemetery, but with no headstone remaining. The sons of George H and Mary Ann Cobby, who owned a fruit store at 105 Spring Bank, which was situated next door to a Presbyterian Church.[60] This church, lay between Park Street and Clarendon Street and was demolished in 1966. The brothers' father,

---

[60] P.45, David Neave.

George H. Cobby, died in 1905, leaving his widow to continue running the fruit store. The whole family were members of the adjacent Church.

Fig.42. The Cobby's shop next to the Presbyterian Church on Spring Bank. Now the site of a Kwik-Fit garage.

Walter was born 1886, and served in the 7th Training TR/5/24215 of the East Yorkshire Regiment and lived at 112 Spring Bank. Walter died on the 3rd November 1916. He is remembered on the memorial in Hull's Northern Cemetery.

Walter's younger brother, Ernest, was born 1890, and enrolled in the Royal Gunner Artillery. Before enlisting he worked as a clerk with the North Eastern Railway. Ernest unfortunately contracted tuberculosis in 1916, aggravated by his military service, and was discharged from the Army in February 1917 as 'no longer physically fit'. He lived at 6 Granville Street after his discharge and was admitted to the Cottingham Sanatorium, where he eventually succumbed to the disease on the 19th February 1918.

Captain William Donaldson was born in Hull in 1881, and became a merchant seaman, mainly employed by the Wilson Line. He married Isobel Rogers at St. Barnabas Church, situated on the corner of the Boulevard and Hessle Road in 1905, and had 3 children. His residence in Hull, where he had been living with his family before his untimely death, was 38 De La Pole Avenue, Spring Bank West.

During his wartime service, he was a member of the crew on board the *S.S. 'Vasco'*, a merchant vessel that struck a mine, dropped from the German submarine UC-16, about 10 miles off Beachy Head on the 16th November 1916. The total loss of life was 17 crew members.

S.S. 'Vasco', built by Furness, Withy & Co. Ltd., West Hartlepool in 1895 and owned at the time of her loss by T. Wilson, Sons & Co. Ltd., Hull, was a British steamer of 1.914 tons and was 280 x 40 x 19.2 feet.

Lieutenant Adrian Farrell served with the 4th Battalion, East Yorkshire Regiment during the Great War. He was born in 1892 and was the son of Thomas Frederic Farrell, a successful local solicitor and Mary Monica Farrell, nee Collingwood, and the family lived at 1 Brookside, Newland Park, Hull. In 1914, this area was just being developed and the two houses called Brookside were some of the first to be erected. His neighbour at 2, Brookside was John Walker Stather, managing director of the Stather Wallpaper Company, and the one of the founders of the Hull Geological Society. Both houses were demolished in the 1960's and a new development now stands on this site.

Fig.43. William Donaldson's headstone.

Adrian attended Hymers College, and passed his law exams, although he went to work at Blundell, Spence & Co as a chemist. Along with two of his brothers, Bede and Wilfred Jerome, he joined the Army in the Great War. He enlisted in the same regiment as his brother, Captain Bede Farrell, who was killed during the 2nd battle of Ypres at Potije Chateau, north of Ypres, on 24th April 1915. Adrian was also severely wounded in the neck, arms and legs in the same battle.

Bede Farrell.

Fig.44. Captain Bede Farrell's image taken from his obituary.

Bede Farrell is commemorated at the Menin Gate Memorial in Ypres, where he is buried. Adrian was returned to England for medical treatment and had several operations on his wounds over the next few months. Eventually released from hospital he returned to the family home in Newland Park and recuperated for over a year.

However, he still had shrapnel in his leg, which had begun to cause septicaemia. Eventually it was decided that amputation was necessary, but during the operation to remove his leg, Adrian sadly died on 23rd August 1916 at the Queen Alexandra Military Hospital in Grosvenor Rd, London.

He was buried with full military honours at the Hull General Cemetery. Strangely, there is currently no headstone nor any mention of him in the Monumental Inscription Books that the East Yorkshire Family History Society have issued relating to Hull General Cemetery.

Lieut. Adrian Farrell.

IMPRESSIVE MILITARY FUNERAL.

Full military honours were accorded to-day to the remains of the late Lieut. Adrian Farrell, 4th East Yorks. Regt., son of Mr and Mrs T. F. Farrell, Brookside, Newland Park, who died from wounds following an operation on Wednesday, in Queen Alexandra's Military Hospital, Millbank, London.

Deceased, who was 24 years of age, was employed in the laboratory of Messrs Blundell, Spence, and Co., as an analytical chemist, at the time of the outbreak of the war, and he enlisted in the 4th East Yorks. After a few months he was given a commission, and in 1915 left England, under the late Colonel Shaw, for active service in Flanders. It will be recalled that Colonel Shaw was killed, and among the officers who lost their lives was Captain Bede Farrell, a brother. Deceased himself received wounds in the same action, from which he never recovered, and he died on Wednesday morning after an operation in the hospital.

Fig.45. Report of Adrian Farrell's funeral.

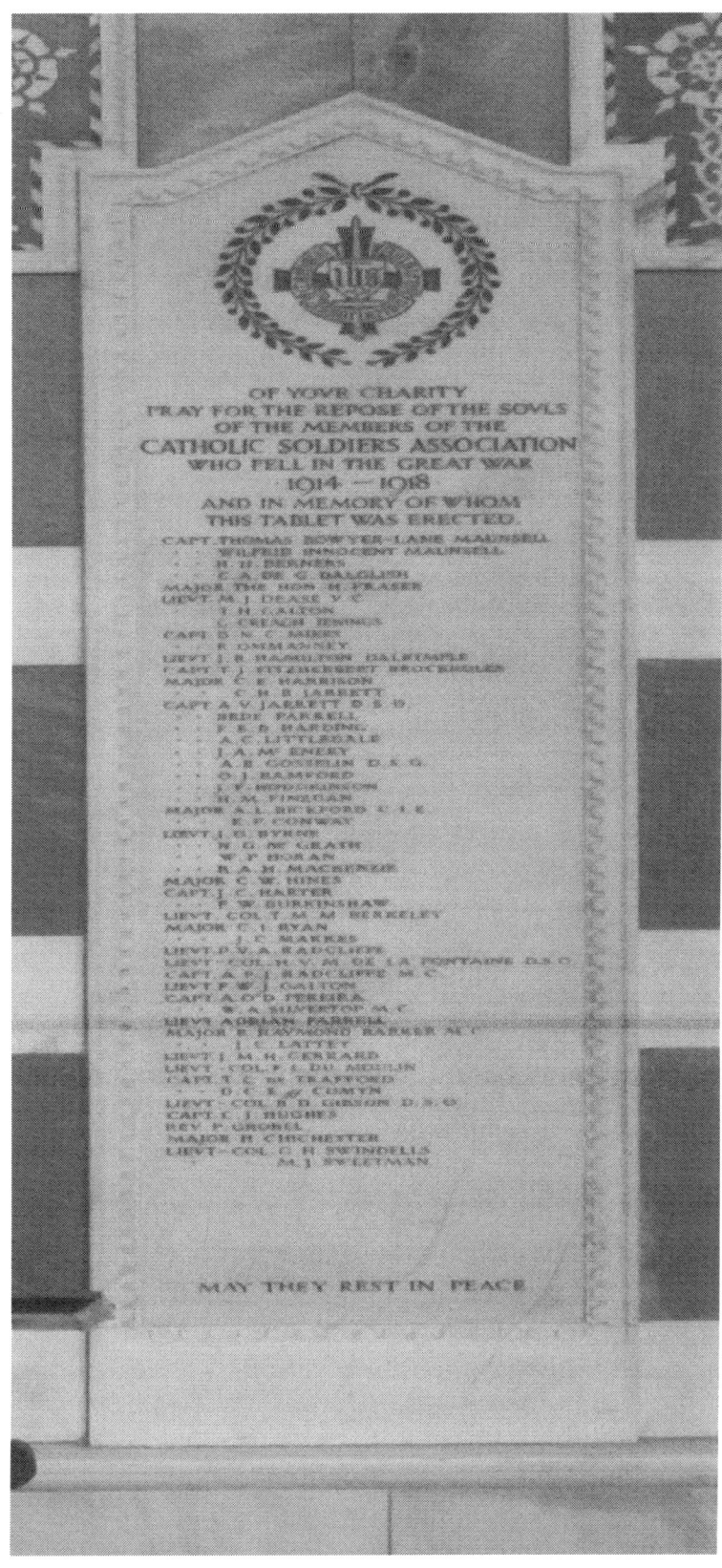

Fig.46. Memorial of Catholic Officers who fell in the Great War in Westminster Chapel of St George, Catholic Soldiers Association Tablets in Victoria Street, London.

His father, Thomas Frederic, and his mother Mary Monica, are also buried in the cemetery and their grave still exists. One of his other brothers, Gilbert Valentine Farrell, survived the Great War, but was killed whilst serving in the Army in 1942 (see separate listing in the World War Two section). Adrian is listed on the Blundell, Spence & Co Memorial plaque and the St. Charles Borromeo memorial plaque in Charles Street. He is also listed on the plaques in Westminster Chapel of St George recording the death of Catholic Officers.

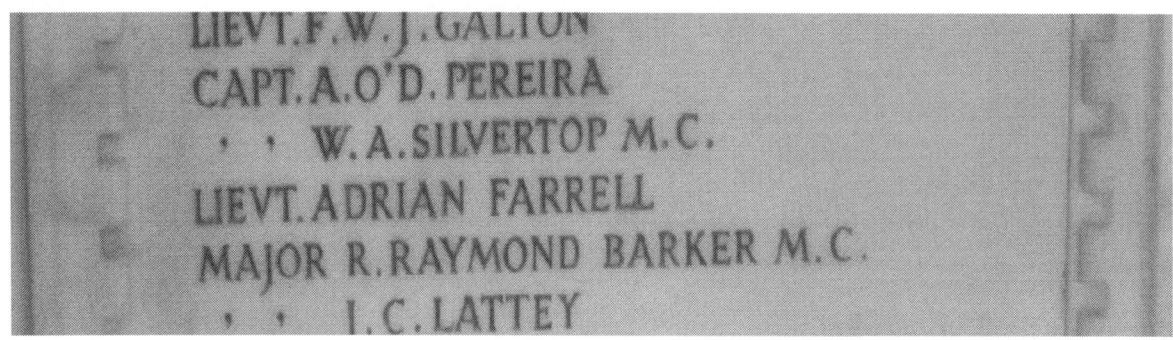

Fig.47. Close up of the image above showing Adrian Farrell's name.

Sergeant T/1273 John Hodgson served with the 130th (Light) Mobile Workshop RAOC. He was born in Hull in 1891 and was raised by his grandparents in the Clifton Street area of Hull. He worked as a carter on a farm at Leconfield. He was discharged from the army as no longer fit for active service, and lived with his wife, Nellie, at 5 Berkley Terrace, Convent Lane, which is now subsumed under the flats on the south side of Anlaby Road, until his death on the 15th June 1920.

Private 10/166 John Hodgson of the 14th Battalion, East Yorkshire Regiment, was born in Hull in 1894. His parents were John Henry and Clara Fanny Hodgson. John was a draper at Hudson, Smith & Co in King Street, and lived with his parents at 139 De Grey Street prior to his enlistment. On the 8th August 1916 he was diagnosed as having an abscess on the mesenteric glands, and was discharged as medically unfit for service. He died whilst at Whittington Barracks, Lichfield on the 9th September 1916, from a tumour on the spine. He is buried in the family grave with his parents, and is the only serviceman to have an official Imperial War Memorial in the Hull General Cemetery.

Fig.48. Sergeant Hodgson.

Fig.49. The sole remaining IWGC headstone left in the Hull General Cemetery.

Fig.50.Thomas Roy Holden.

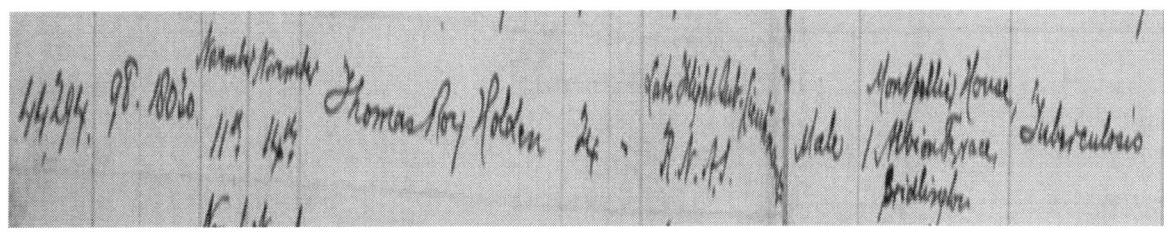

Fig.51. The burial record for Thomas Roy Holden.

THE LATE FLIGHT-LIEUT. HOLDEN

MILITARY HONOURS AT THE FUNERAL.

A fitting tribute was paid, at the General Cemetery, Hull, this afternoon, the remains of Mr Thomas Roy Holden, formerly a second-lieutenant in the East Yorks Regiment, and late Flight Sub-Lieutenant, R.N.A.S., elder son of Mr Thomas Holden, jun., of Bishop-mansions, London. Deceased was the grandson of Mr Thomas Holden, head of the firm of Messrs Holden, Sons, and Hodgson, solicitors, of Trinity House-lane, Hull.

The death took place at Bridlington on Saturday under sad circumstances. Deceased commenced a promising career in the office of Messrs Holden, Sons, and Hodgson, of Hull, and later was articled with the firm of Messrs Nicholson, Graham, and Jones, solicitors, of London. At the beginning of the war he enlisted in the East Yorks Regiment, and was exceedingly popular among the local officers and men. After eight months' training he was invalided out of the regiment in consequence of an internal ailment, but on making what, it was hoped, was a satisfactory recovery, he re-enlisted and joined the Royal Naval Air Service. He soon gained his certificate, and received commission of a flight sub-lieutenant. Before long he had an accident, as a consequence of which there was a recurrence of his previous ailment, which caused him to be again invalided out of the Service. He gradually got worse, and died on Saturday at the age of 24.

The remains were brought from Bridlington this morning on a motor car to Wenlock Barracks, for the purpose of the remains being accorded military honours. The coffin was conveyed on a gun carriage, and it was covered by the Union Jack. On the gun carriage lay also beautiful floral tributes from the Admiralty and the Military authorities. The 2nd Garrison Battalion, East Yorkshire Regiment, furnished the firing party, which was in charge of Lieut Sharman, and a bearer party was formed of six sergeants of the E.Y. 2nd Garrison Battalion, to which deceased formerly belonged. The band of the 3rd East Yorkshire Battalion attended and played the "Dead March" as the cortege neared the General Cemetery.

Fig.52. Report of Thomas Holden's funeral in Hull General Cemetery.

Flight Sub-Lieutenant Thomas Roy Holden was born in 1892 at Albion House, Willerby to Thomas Holden & Mabel Constance (Lamb). His father was a partner in the solicitors' firm of Holden Sons & Hodgson, who had offices in Bowlalley Lane and later, Trinity House Lane. His mother died in 1897 and Thomas lived with the Hodgson family, who were his relatives, at Scarborough House, Beverley. Thomas was articled as a solicitor to a law firm in London.

When war broke out he enlisted in the East Yorkshire Regiment as a 2nd Lieutenant, but was invalided out due to a long-standing chest infection. Still wanting to do his patriotic duty, he then joined the Royal Naval Air Service as a Flight Sub-Lieutenant. However, he had a plane crash and his chest complaint returned. He went to live at Montpelier House in Bridlington to recuperate, but sadly died of tuberculosis on the 11th November 1916, aged 24.

He was given a full military funeral at Hull General Cemetery, however, his headstone no longer remains, but we do know the compartment and grave number, which is 98/18030. He is not listed on the CWGC site, and has no known memorial.

Private 3/6962 William Henry Hotchkin, was born in 1874, so by the time the Great War was declared he was already a veteran soldier. He had served with the Lincolnshire Regiment and had fought in the Boer War. After discharge from the Army he returned to his job as a baker, and later re-joined the East Yorkshire Regiment on the outbreak of the Great War. He was the son of William and Jane Hotchkin of 15 Reed St, Hull and was the husband of Ada Wade Hotchkin of 17 Ockley Terrace, West Parade, Hull. He was eventually transferred to the Labour Corps, probably due to his age. He died on the 9th March 1918.

Lieutenant Colonel Col Richard Ethelbert Johnson of the RGA (Volunteers) and late of the East Yorkshire Regiment, was born in Hull in 1856. He was articled to Thomas Ward Hearfield, solicitors of Hull and he had his own legal practice at St Mary's Chambers, Lowgate. He married Kate Kay in 1883 and had eight children, living at Balmoral Terrace on Anlaby Rd, which was a very fashionable part of town. One of his near neighbours would have been John Fountain, who, was not only an important town councillor, but also Chairman of the Guardians of the Poor and Governor of the Hull Workhouse. Balmoral Terrace stood in between West Parade and Arlington Street and the site is now occupied by Hull and East Yorkshire Women and Children's Hospital. The house was later renumbered as 164 Anlaby Rd.

Richard himself had a seat on the board of The Victoria Children's Hospital, and was also a Major in the 2nd East Riding of Yorkshire RGA (Volunteers), a position from which he retired in 1899. At the outbreak of the Great War, he volunteered his services, and was given the rank of a Lieutenant Colonel in the same regiment. Whilst attending a function of the RGA Regiment, at the Station Hotel, in Goole, he suddenly collapsed and died at the age of 59. He was given a full military funeral at Hull General Cemetery, and is buried in the family grave there. His son, Albert Kay Johnson, was a gunner in the Canadian Field Artillery and was killed in France in 1918. (see later entry).

Fig.53. Private Hotchkin.

Fig.54. Colonel Johnson's monument, 2018.

Lieutenant and Quartermaster Vincent Knowles, of the Royal Engineers was a career soldier, born in Immingham in 1862 and lived at 76 Blenheim Street, Princes Avenue, Hull, in the new development of its time that was to become known as the 'Dukeries'. He died on 14th October 1915, aged 53, and is buried in The Hull General Cemetery, but with no known headstone or monumental inscription, although he is remembered on the panel in Northern Cemetery. His son Gordon Knowles also served in the army in the Great War.

Bombardier 290044 Arthur Marr of the 24th Siege Battery RGA, born in Hull in 1889, lived at 79 Constable Street, on Hessle Road with his parents, Thomas and Eleanor Marr. Arthur was a printer and unmarried, and survived the war. However, a greater killer was stalking the world in the aftermath of the Great War and that was the Influenza pandemic of 1918-1919. Arthur was one of the victims of it. He died at the family home from influenza, ironically and sadly, only one day after the war had ceased.

Private 29530 George Frederick Walter Spence of the 7th Battalion, East Yorkshire Regiment, was the son of Fred and Florence Spence. He was born in Hull in 1899. His mother had died in 1905. They had lived at 11 Washington Street on Beverley Road but after his mother died, Arthur's father married again, and the family moved to 21 Alexandra Road, Beverley Road. Arthur's father was a master mariner, and before joining up at the age of 17, George had been an apprentice painter.

George suffered gunshot wounds in May 1918, and was invalided home, seriously injured, and sadly died soon after, at the Southwark Military Hospital in London.

Trimmer 6399 TS RNR Gilbert West was born in Ophir, Central Otago, New Zealand on 31st December 1891. He came to England around 1905 and married Annie Smith at St Mary & St Peter's Church, Dairycoates, on 12th June 1916. He served as a trimmer on the shore-based *H.M.S. Acteon* in Sheerness, Kent. He also contracted influenza at the end of the war and he too died, just one day after the war ended, in Chatham Naval Hospital on 12th November 1918.

Fig.55. The burial record of Gilbert West.

1b. The Second World War

Flight Sergeant 1073431 Frederick Cyril Baker served with the RAF Volunteer Reserve. He was born in Hull in 1921, the son of Frances Baker and the stepson of John Morrison, and lived at 38 Reldene Drive, Willerby Road. He joined the RAF upon the outbreak of war, where he became a Wireless Operator/Air Gunner. He died, along with the other three crew members on the 28th December 1941, when the Bristol Beaufort 1 N106 he was flying, crashed at South Coombe Farm, Stoke Climsland, Devon, whilst returning from a training sortie. The investigation into the accident reported that the port engine had stopped, and the aircraft crashed and was completely burnt out. There were no survivors.

Aircraftman 2nd Class 552565 Ernest Duff was also born in Hull in 1921, and lived at 46 De La Pole Avenue with his widowed mother, Christine (Rainey). Ernest was serving with 97 Squadron at R.A.F. Abingdon. On the 8th September 1939, his Armstrong Whitworth Whitley B Mk2 bomber, number K7225, was returning to base when the pilot, who was flying too low, hit a tree and crashed into a house, killing all three crew.

Private 13028214 Harold Evers was born in Hull in 1906. He worked as an artificial stone mason and had married Lily Nichols at the Hull Register Office in 1933. From this marriage they had a daughter, Sheila, and the family lived at 286 Wold Road. He served with the Auxiliary Military Pioneer Corps and died at Broadgreen Hospital, Liverpool on 6th August 1940.

Major 107625 Gilbert Valentine Farrell born in Hull in 1884, was the son of Thomas and Monica Farrell, and brother of Adrian and Bede Farrell, both of whom died in the Great War. Major Farrell served in the Indian Army in the Great War, and re-enlisted in the Army at the outbreak of the Second World War in 1939. He was given a commission in the Pioneer Corps.

He married Dorothy Sherburn, the daughter of Alderman Sherburn of Brantinghamthorpe Hall, and lived in Tonbridge, Kent. He died in the Emergency Hospital at Great Barr on 11th August 1942. He was buried in one of the Farrell family plots in the adjacent grave to his brother Adrian.

Private D/22916 James Hargreaves was born in Hull in 1890, the son of Joseph and Ann Hargreaves, and lived at 8 Warneford Terrace, Stanley Street. He served with the 6th (HD) Battalion, East Yorkshire Regiment, and died of pneumonia at the Hull Royal Infirmary Annexe situated at Withernsea, on the 1st December 1939.

Merchant Seaman Sydney Hutton was born in Hull in 1879. His parents were the local fish merchant, Thomas Hutton, and his wife Kate. Initially, Sydney worked on trawlers, where he gained his mates' certificate, and later his masters' certificate allowing him to captain the long-haul shipping that sailed to foreign parts. He worked on ocean going vessels for the Wilson Line. He married Matilda Hudson in 1920 and lived at 9 Clumber Street.

Fig.56. Sydney Hutton's Masters' Certificate.

CODING 241 500 659 B 51 40 3 241 | 1 | G.R. 288

Nat. | Rank or Rating | Cause of Death | Ship | Age Group | Date of Death | Res. | R of H List Number

Record of Death of Merchant Seaman

Surname: HUTTON Ship: SS "Albano"

Other Names: Sydney Official No: 133420

Address: 9. Clumber Street Hull (N/K - Wife - Matilda - S/A) Port of Registry: Hull

British/~~Fishing/Foreign~~

Birthplace: Hull Country: England Rank or Rating: Master (M)

Date of Death: 2.3.40 Place of Death: At Sea Age at Death: 51.

Cause of Death: Supposed drowned thro' mining and sinking of S.S. Albano

Ppd by: Ckd by: Registry Entry: Year: 1940 Month: April Page: 6. C.A. 1

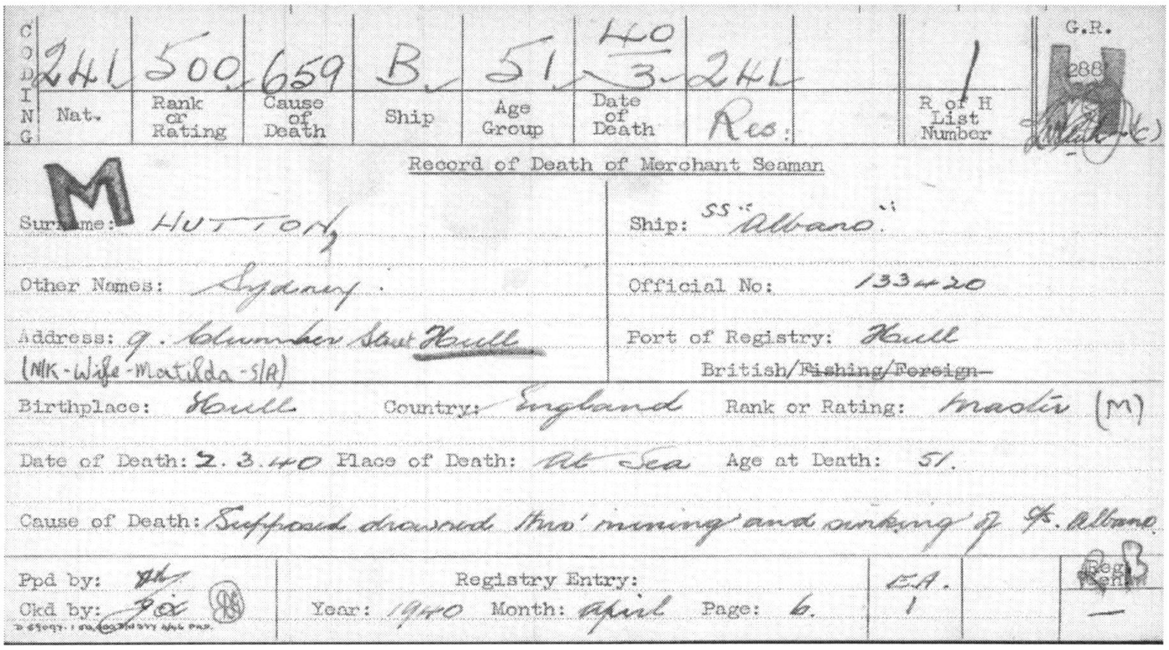

Fig.57. Sydney Hutton's Record of Death.

During the war he was the Master of the Wilson Line ship *S.S. 'Albano',* when it struck a mine and sank, 4 miles off Sunderland on the 2nd March 1940. Sydney and eight other crewmen lost their lives.

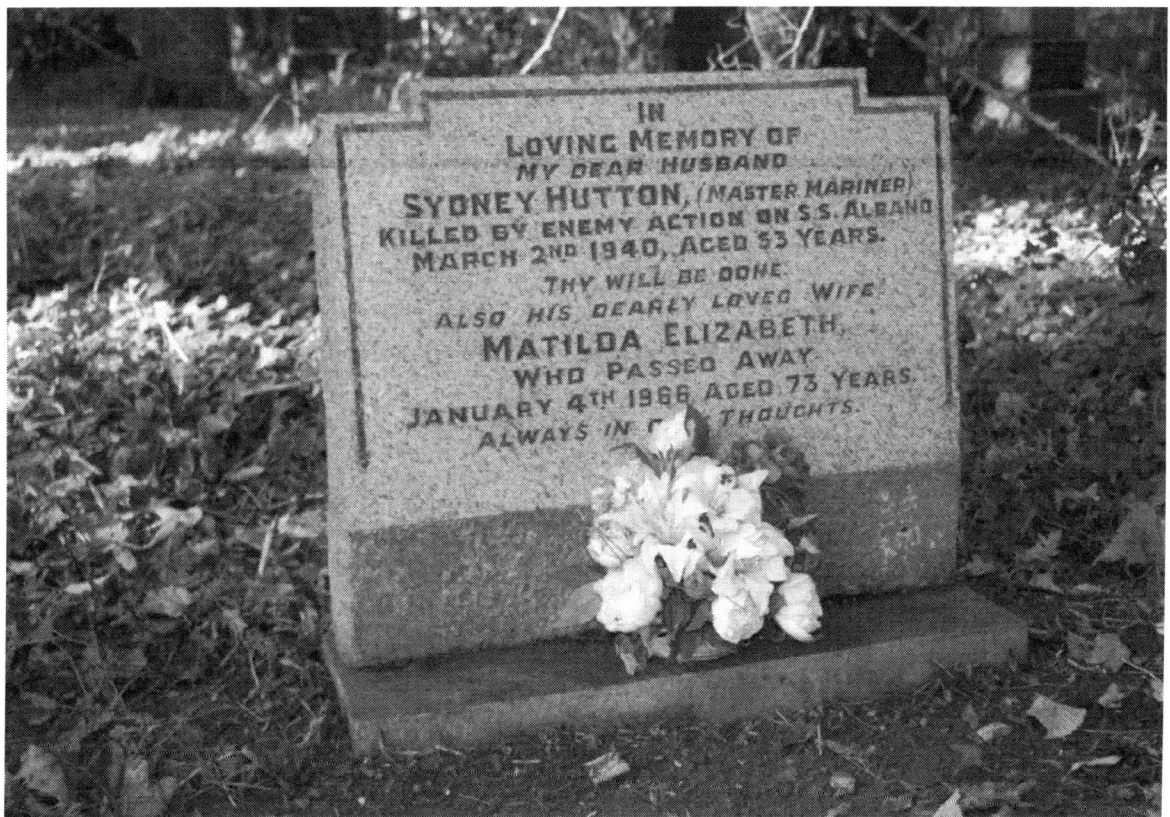

Fig.58. Hutton's headstone, 2018.

Private 13088955 Joseph Mundy Kemp was born in Hull in 1910, and worked as a Paint Grinder. He married May French in 1934, and lived initially at 153 English Street, but later moved to 12 Melbourne Terrace, Bean Street. He served with the Pioneer Corps, and was taken Prisoner of War, but sadly, after repatriation, he died at the Joint Isolation Hospital at Axbridge, Somerset on 17th February 1943.

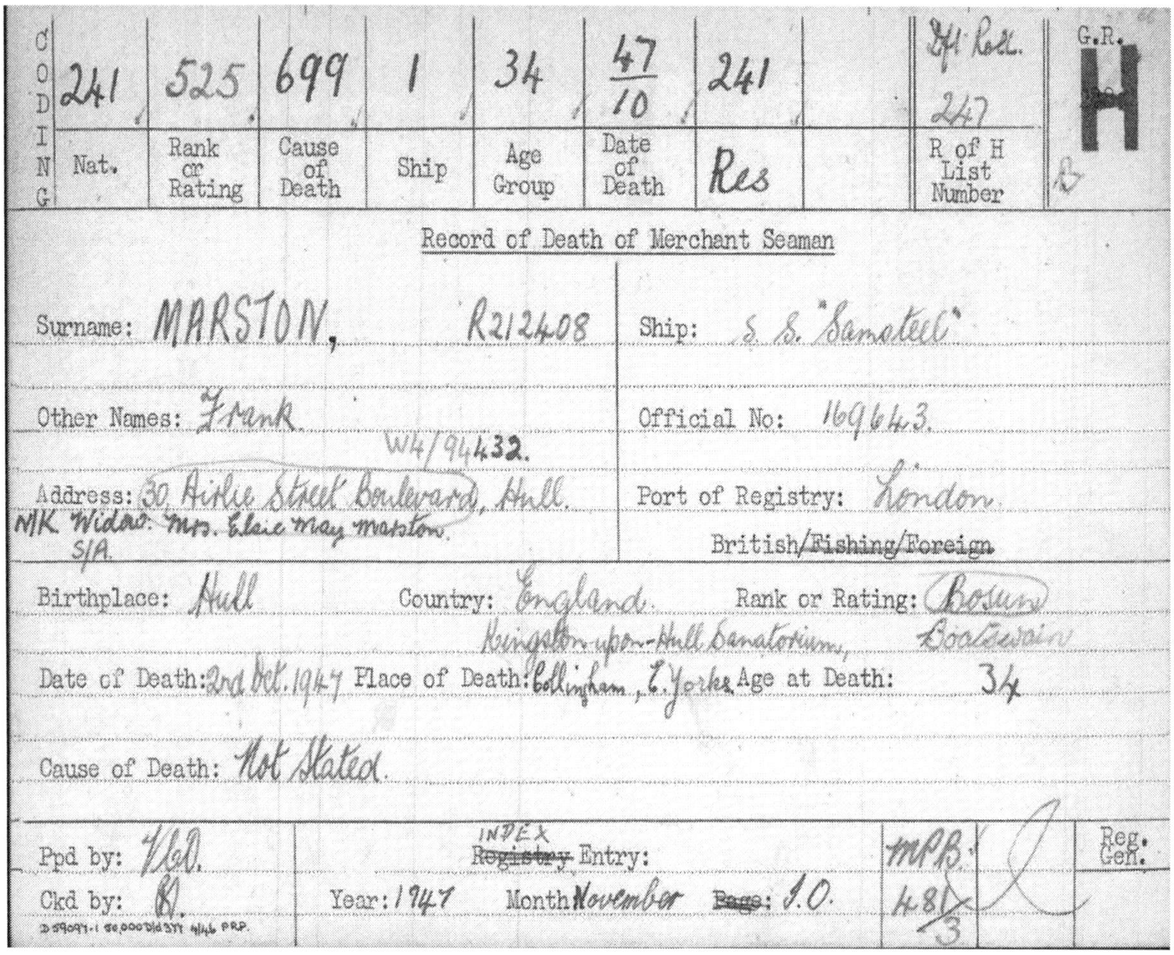

CODING	Nat.	Rank or Rating	Cause of Death	Ship	Age Group	Date of Death	Res		R of H List Number	G.R.
	241	525	699	1	34	47/10	241		247	H

Record of Death of Merchant Seaman

Surname: MARSTON, R212408 | Ship: S. S. "Samsteel"

Other Names: Frank W4/94432. | Official No: 169643.

Address: 30, Airlie Street Boulevard, Hull. | Port of Registry: London.

N/K Widow: Mrs. Elsie May Marston. S/A.

British/~~Fishing/Foreign~~

Birthplace: Hull Country: England. Rank or Rating: Bosun Boatswain

Date of Death: 2nd Oct. 1947 Place of Death: Kingston-upon-Hull Sanatorium, Cottingham, E. Yorks Age at Death: 34

Cause of Death: Not Stated.

Ppd by: | ~~Registry~~ INDEX Entry: | MPB | Reg. Gen.

Ckd by: | Year: 1947 Month November ~~Page~~: 1.0. | 481/3

Fig.59. Frank Marston's Record of Death.

Boatswain Frank Marston was born in Hull in 1913, and was a career seaman, sailing on ocean going vessels. He married Elsie May Dye in 1942 and lived at 80 Airlie Street. During the war he was serving aboard the Liberty ship *'S.S. Samsteel'* when he contracted an illness. He was transported back home to Britain but died at Cottingham Sanatorium on the 2nd October 1947.

Private 14219902 Harry Trevor Mather was born in Hull in 1924 to George and Annie Mather (nee Balderson). The family lived at 2 King Street in the centre of the old town, within sight of Holy Trinity Church. He served with the Durham

Light Infantry, and was living at 33 Gwendwr Road, Fulham, when he was killed in an air raid that struck the house on the 20th February 1944.

	1 NAME (Surname first)	2 PORT DIVISION and OFFICIAL NO.	3 BRANCH OF SERVICE	4 RATING	5 SHIP OR UNIT	6 DATE OF BIRTH	7 PLACE OF BIRTH	8 DATE OF DEATH	9 CAUSE OF DEATH	10 PLACE OF DEATH	11 DECORATIONS (If any)
1	MAVOR, Robert George Innes	FAA/FX 76081	R.N.	A/Ldg. Air Mech. (O)	H.M.S. ARCHER	1.5.1919	St. George, Edinburgh	19.6.1942	1	At Sea	
2	MAW, George	C/JX 319963	R.N.	Ord. Seaman	H.M.S. PHOEBE	25.5.1925	Doncaster, Yorks	23.10.1942	1	At Sea	
3	MAW, William George	P/JX 201286	R.N.	Ord. Seaman	H.M.S. MANISTEE	22.4.1920	Sunderland, Durham	24.2.1941	2	At Sea	
4	MAWBY, Kenneth Roger	PLY/X 1421	R.M.	Marine	H.M.S. GLOUCESTER	20.10.1918	Rugby, Warwick	22.5.1941	2	Crete	
5	MAWBY, Peter	P/JX 145116	R.N.	A/Ldg. Seaman	H.M.S. CAMPBELTOWN	6.3.1919	Grantham, Lincs	28.3.1942	2	At Sea	
6	MAWDSLEY, Reginald	P/JX 282987	R.N.	A.B.	H.M.S. HURWORTH	17.8.1920	Coppull, Lancs	22.10.1943	2	At Sea	
7	MAWDSLEY, Arthur Thomas	D/MD/X 2775	R.N.V.R.	A.B.	H.M.S. MAHRATTA	24.10.1919	Liverpool, Lancs	25.2.1944	2	At Sea	
8	MAWDSLEY, John	C/JX 355104	R.N.	A.B.	H.M. L.S.T. 421	25.11.1923	Leigh, Lancs	26.1.1944	1	At Sea	
9	MAWDSLEY, John Dale	C/JX 287485	R.N.	A/A.B.	H.M.S. PRESIDENT III - S.S. ALHAMA	6.4.1907	Bootle, Lancs	7.12.1941	1	Military Hospital, Londonderry	
10	MAWE, Harry	C/JX 251224	R.N.	Ord. Coder	H.M.S. GALATEA	8.6.1922	Sheffield, Yorks	15.12.1941	2	At Sea	
11	MAWE, Peter Geoffrey	RTE/R 269653	T.124 T	Fireman	H.M.S. MINONA	22.8.1924	Hull, Yorks	31.12.1944	3 Chronic Parenchymatous Nephritis	R.N.Hospital, Hull, Yorks	
12	MAWHINNEY, Henry	P/ESD/X 1690	R.N.V.R.	A.B.	H.M.S. PUCKERIDGE	15.11.1919	Dundee, Angus	6.9.1943	2	At Sea	

Fig.60. Record of death of Peter Mawe.

Able Seaman Peter Geoffrey Mawe was also born in Hull in 1924, the son of Mr. Austin Wilfred Mawe and his wife Dora, and lived at 19 The Greenway, North Road. He enlisted in the Royal Navy and was a fireman with the Naval Auxiliary Personnel on board *H.M.S. 'Minona'* and *H.M. Rescue Tug 'Griffin'*. He died at a

Hull Naval Hospital, of chronic liver disease, on the 31st December 1944, aged only 20.

Fig.61. Shell-Mex Building to the left on the newly built Ferensway in the 1930's.

Fig.62. The same building after the bombing.

Aircraftman 2nd Class 21025769 Otto Fowler Meggitt was born in Hull in 1921. He was the son of Samuel and Ethel Meggitt, who lived at 24 Gladstone Street, prior to moving to 129 Kingston Road, Willerby. Otto was in the R.A.F. Volunteer Reserve, and on the evening of the 31st March 1941, during the blitz on Hull, he was in the recently built Shell-Mex building on Ferensway, which was being utilized as the A.R.P. Headquarters. Around 11.30 that night, a mine fell about 20 yards from the building, on a derelict site that older readers may remember as the site of the Locarno, and later LA's nightclub. It is now the site of the Hilton Hotel. The Shell-Mex building was badly damaged, and seven people, including Otto, lost their lives that night. He is commemorated on the People's Memorial in Paragon St.

Chief Engineer Ernest Roberts was born in Southampton in 1884 and worked as a marine engineer. He married Eva Crowe in Hull in 1914 and lived at 21 Louis Street. During the war he was the Chief Engineer with the Merchant Navy on board the *'S.S. Lorient'* (Cardiff), which was a French built ship that was captured by the British whilst being used by the Vichy Government. He died at home on 4th April 1942 from what was noted as a 'war risk injury'.

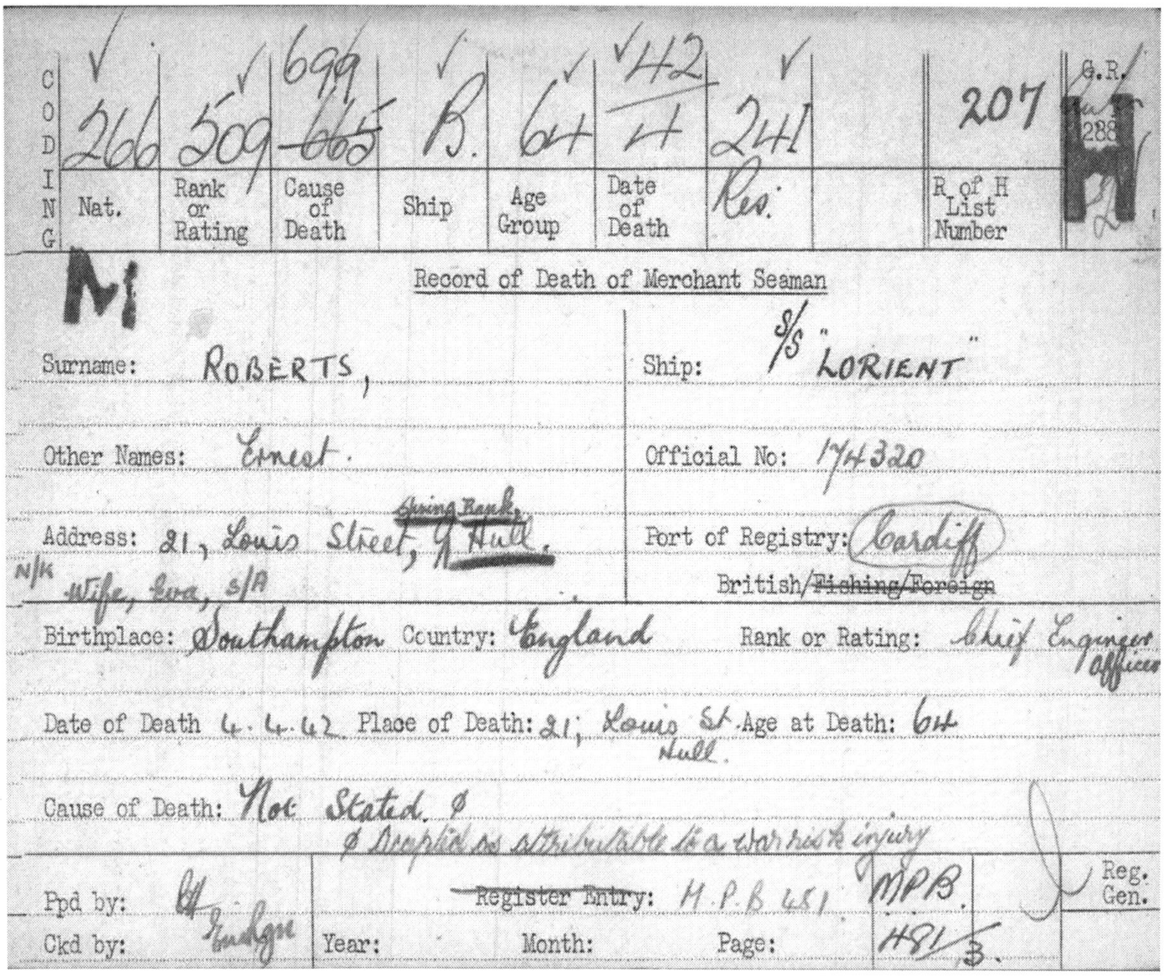

CODING	Nat.	Rank or Rating	Cause of Death	Ship	Age Group	Date of Death		R of H List Number	G.R.
	266	509	699 ~~665~~	B.	64	42/4	241 Res.	207	288

Record of Death of Merchant Seaman

Surname: ROBERTS,
Ship: S/S "LORIENT"

Other Names: Ernest.
Official No: 174320

Address: 21, Louis Street, ~~Spring Bank, Hull.~~
N/K Wife, Eva, s/a
Port of Registry: Cardiff
British/~~Fishing/Foreign~~

Birthplace: Southampton Country: England Rank or Rating: Chief Engineer Officer

Date of Death 4.4.42 Place of Death: 21, Louis St. Hull. Age at Death: 64

Cause of Death: Not Stated. ø
ø Accepted as attributable to a war risk injury

Ppd by: ~~Register Entry~~: M.P.B 481 MPB. Reg. Gen.
Ckd by: Year: Month: Page: 481 3.

Fig.63. Record of Death for Chief Engineer Roberts.

Captain 46441 George Shetliff Wood was born in Hull in 1891, the son of Captain George Edmund and Lucy Wood of 33 Victoria Avenue. The family later moved to Avenue Halcyon, Hessle. George Shetliff trained as an electrical engineer, and married Clara May Jones at St Augustine's Church, on Queen's Road, Hull in 1916. They moved to the 'The Cottage', Ashlett Road, Fawley in the New Forest, where he worked as a general foreman at an oil refinery. He was given a commission as a Lieutenant in the Army. During the war he was promoted to Captain in the Royal Engineers. He died whilst at The Clifton Court in Bristol on 16th February 1944. His cremated remains were buried on the 16th May 1944 in the family vault which still exists.

Fig.64. Shetliff's monument, 2018.

Private 4618983 Arthur Wrigglesworth was born in Hull in 1919. He lived at 1 Villa Terrace, Alexandra Street. He served with the Duke of Wellington's Regiment (West Riding), and died at Loughborough District Hospital 1st July 1941.

2. Men who were not buried in the cemetery, but have remaining memorials.

Two brothers who died in the Great War that are buried in France but have a headstone in Hull General Cemetery are:

Private 9/21908 Ernest Dixon of the 10th East Yorkshire Regiment was born in 1896. He was hit by a high explosive shell at Oppy Wood and died on the 25th June 1917.

Private 13957 Harold Dixon of 6th East Yorkshire Regiment was born in 1893 and killed in action on the 26th September 1916.

Fig.65. The Dixon brothers' headstone in Hull General Cemetery.

They were two of eleven children who were born to John Robert and Christina Dixon (nee Watson) of 78 Manchester Street. One of their other brothers, Arthur Dixon, served with the Northumberland Fusiliers and Yorkshire and Lancashire Regiment. He was severely wounded in France in 1916, but survived the war, and lived with his wife Phoebe at 7 Humber Avenue, Rugby Street, later moving to Scarborough where he died in 1965.

2nd Lieutenant Arthur Godman Jones of the 10th East Yorkshire, known as the 'Commercials', as they were one of the 'Pals' battalions, recruited from office workers. He was the youngest son of Robert Thomas and Mary A Jones who lived at 54, Sunnybank.

He attended the Hull Grammar School and was remembered on the memorial plaques that were in the school vestibule at the site in Bishop Alcock Road which has now been demolished. Arthur was wounded and died in France on the 1st July 1917, aged 36. He was buried in the Duisans British Cemetery, Etrun.

Sergeant 11460 Laurance Steele of the 17th Battalion, West Yorkshire Regiment (Prince of Wales Own), was the son of Thomas Robert and Mary Steele of 369 Beverley Road. He died on 25th April 1916, and is buried at Merville Communal Cemetery, France

Lance Corporal 2415 Michael John Kelly was a Lewis Gunner with the 4th Battalion of the East Yorkshire Regiment and the son of Michael Kelly, Superintendent of Hull General Cemetery, and his wife Susanna Kelly.

He and two of his comrades were killed by a 'minnewerfer' on Easter Day 22nd April 1916, aged 23. He is buried at Lindenhoek Chalet Military Cemetery, near Kemel, West-Vlaanderen.

Fig.66. Michael Kelly's headstone in Lindenhoek Cemetery in Belgium.

Fig.67. Michael J Kelly.

Fig.68. Arthur Godman Jones's monument in Hull General Cemetery.

Fig.69. Sergeant Laurence Steele.

Fig.70. Footstone on Laurence Steele's grave in Hull General Cemetery.

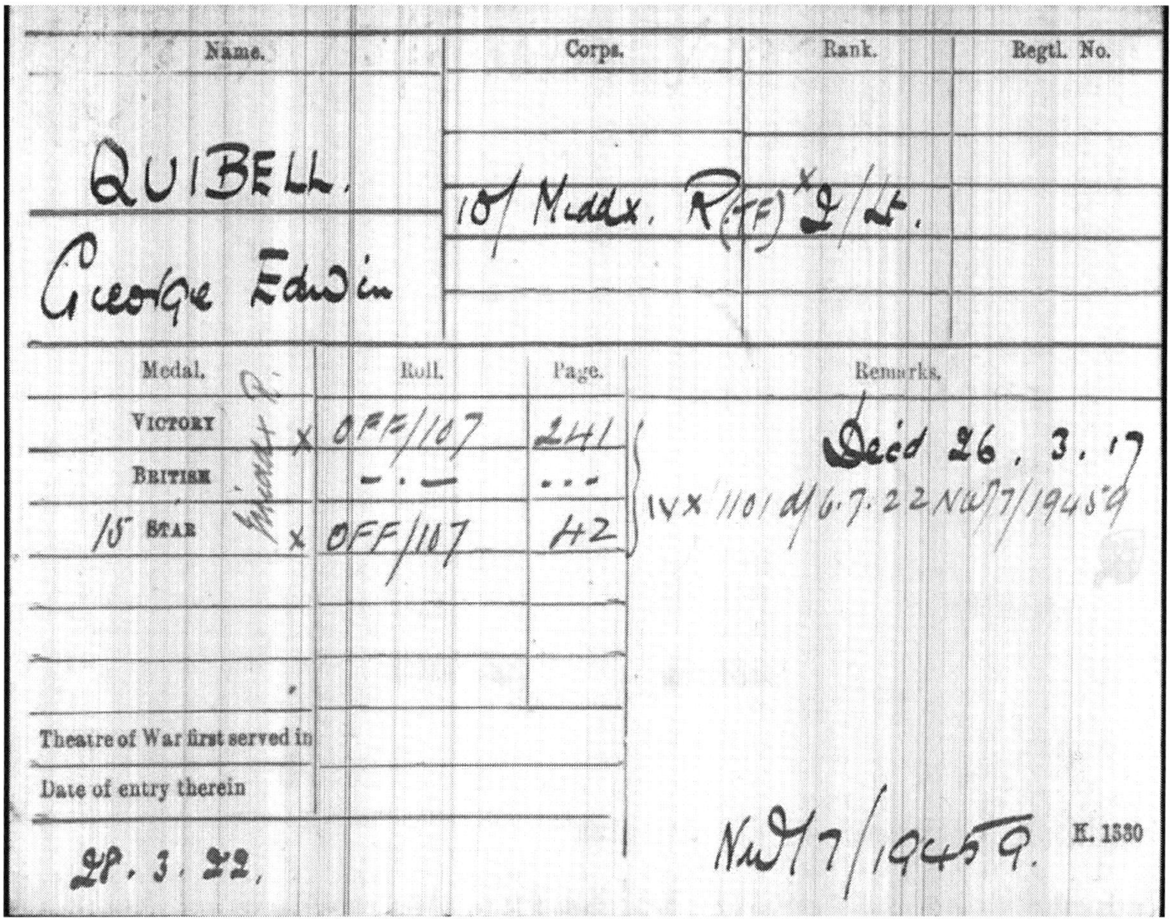

Name. | Corps. | Rank. | Regtl. No.

QUIBELL.
George Edwin
10/ Middx. R. (T.F.) 2/Lt.

Medal.	Roll.	Page.	Remarks.
Victory x	OFF/107	241	Decd 26. 3. 17
British	– . –	. . .	IVX 1101 d/6.7.22 NW/7/19459
15 Star x	OFF/117	42	

Theatre of War first served in
Date of entry therein
28. 3. 22.
NW/7/19459.
K. 1380

Fig.71. The Great War medal card for George Quibell.

2nd Lieutenant George Edwin Quibell served with the 10th Battalion, Middlesex Regiment. He was the son of Edwin and Sophie Elizabeth Quibell, Building Contractor, 11 Fitzroy Street. His regiment was attached to the Egyptian Expeditionary Force and was involved in heavy fighting in Gaza, in what was then Palestine.

During the evening of the 25th March 1917, the battalion moved out from an orchard across a range of hillocks and gullies. The following morning and was misty at 11.40 a.m. on the 26th, they were involved in heavy fire. Lieutenant Quibell had his back pack blasted off with a shell, but continued to lead his men, eventually falling. He was listed as being killed on the 26th March 1917 and is commemorated on the Jerusalem Memorial.

Fig.72. George Quibell in the Great War.

Fig.73. George's headstone in Hull General Cemetery.

Gunner 294825 Joseph Hall served with the 30th Siege Battery RGA. He was the son of John William and Catherine Hall, shoemaker and boot repairer of 25 Waterhouse Lane. He was killed in action 7th October 1917, and was buried at the Menin Road Military Cemetery, Ypres.

Lieutenant Frederick Vincent Hall served with the 210th Squadron, R.A.F. He was the son of Frederick William and Florence Elizabeth Hall, Oaklands Park, Tolleshunk Knights, Essex. He won the Dunkirk Medal for bravery and his actions are recorded on a wall plaque in the local church, where his parents were buried. He died on the 15th May 1917. He is buried in Ebblinghem Military Cemetery, France.

Fig.74. Frederick Vincent Hall in his RFC uniform.

Fig.75. Vincent Hall's headstone in Hull General Cemetery.

Fig.76.Thomas Margerison.

2nd Lieutenant Thomas Margerison served with the 1st Huntingdon Cyclist Battalion, that was attached to the R.F.C. He lost his life whilst in aerial combat on the 13th April 1917, aged 22, and was buried in Brown's Copse Cemetery, Roeux, France.

Fig.77. The Margerison headstone showing both of the family members who lost their lives in the Great War.

Fig.78. The Margerison headstone, 2018.

George William Margerison was a 3rd Officer in the Merchant Navy. Born in Leeds, and the son of Walter and Jane Margerison, (nee Walton). They lived at 18 Goddard Avenue, Hull. He was killed in action on the Wilson Line ship *S.S. 'Chicago'* off Flamborough on the 8th July 1918. He is commemorated on the Tower Hill Memorial.

Fig.79.George Margerison

Lance Corporal 10/1291 William Ernest Fowler served with 10th Battalion, East Yorkshire Regiment, 'C' Coy (Commercials). He was the son of Mary Fowler who lived at 112 Plane Street and her late husband Skelton Fowler. William died on the 20th August 1918 aged 34. He is buried at Longuenesse, (St Omer) Souvenir Cemetery.

Private 75917 James Arthur Wilson 1/4 Battalion, Northumberland Fusiliers, was the son of James and Margaret Elizabeth Wilson, confectioner of 43 Queen Street, Hull. He died on the 27th May 1918, aged only 18 years. He is commemorated on the Soissons Memorial in France.

Gunner 322854 Albert Kay Johnson of the 8th Canadian Field Artillery, was born in Hull in 1888, the 3rd son of Mrs Kate Ellen Johnson and the late Colonel Richard Ethelbert Johnson, (see Section 1a). He emigrated to Canada around 1913, and at the outbreak of the Great War he joined the Canadian Field Artillery. He died of wounds in France on the 16th April 1918 aged 29. He is buried at Etaples Military Cemetery, and remembered on the family monument in Hull General Cemetery.

3. Men who were not buried in the cemetery, but originally had memorials in the cemetery

Gunner 143039 Frederick E Saltfleet, RGA, the husband of Esther A. Saltfleet, of 313 South Boulevard, Hull. Frederick died at Ypres on the 28th October 1917 and was buried at the Ypres Town Cemetery Extension. He was originally remembered on a plaque on Captain William Donaldson's grave in Hull General Cemetery but this was later removed.

Private 40024 John Bertram Wardrobe served in the 7th Battalion, East Yorkshire Regiment. He was the son of Arthur Langhorn and Emma Ann Wardrobe, who lived at 2 Percy's Avenue, South Parade. John died on the 4th November 1918, aged 20, and his remains are buried at the Englefontaine British Cemetery, France.

Private 44169 Benjamin Lomax of the Durham Light Infantry was the son of Sarah Jane Lomax and her late husband, Benjamin Lomax. The family lived at 42

Ryde Street, Beverley Road. Benjamin died on the 31st March 1918, aged 27. He is commemorated on the Pozieres Memorial, Somme, France.

Private 4822 Frederick Ingleby served with the 15th Battalion, Australian Infantry, AIF. He died in the Sydney Hospital, Sydney, on the 18th February 1918, aged 36. He is buried at the Rockwood Necropolis, Sydney, New South Wales in Australia.

Private 30525 Herbert Tipple of the 182nd Company (Infantry), Machine Gun Corps, was the son of William and Maria Tipple, Tor Cottage, Stepney Drive, Scarborough. He died on the 19th July 1916, aged 27, and was buried at Cabaret-Rouge British Cemetery, France.

Private 12703 Sidney Webster Gee served with the 7th Battalion, East Yorkshire Regiment. He was the son of Sarah Emma Gee and the late Arthur Gee, of 96 Sunny Bank, Hull. Sydney was killed in action at Bapaume on the 12th November 1916, aged 24. There was originally a foot stone to Arthur Butler Gee's headstone, but this was later removed. He is commemorated on Thiepval Memorial, Somme, France

Private 11031 Joseph Hall of the Honourable Artillery Company, was the son of Thomas Newlove Hall and Sarah Ann Hall, of 2 Fountain Street. He was the husband of Lily Muriel Hall, (nee Stephens) and lived at 344 Fulwood Road, Sheffield. He was killed in action in Italy on the 11th August 1918. He is commemorated on the Giavera Memorial, Italy.

Private 1509 Arthur Fewster of the 5th Battalion, East Yorkshire Regiment, son of George Frederick and Mary Alice Fewster, was killed in action at Ypres on 25th April 1915, aged 20. He is commemorated on the Menin Gate Memorial, Ypres.

Private 867 Reginald Conrad Neill served with the 10th Battalion, East Yorkshire Regiment (Commercials). He was the son of the late Captain Robert Rowley and Alice Neill, originally of 19 Albany Street, Hull. He married and lived with his wife Alice at 11 Stanmore Rd, West Green, London. He died of wounds on the 21st June 1916 and is buried at Abbeville Communal Cemetery, Somme, France

Private 4297/A Frederick Harold Taylor of the Australian Infantry, A.L.F., was the son of Clara Ann Taylor, of Broadgates Hospital, Walkington. Frederick died on the 12th October 1917, aged 29. He is commemorated on the Menin Gate Memorial, Ypres

Gunner 98189 Harold Dawson served with the Heavy Battery, RGA, and was the son of Thomas and Mary Dawson. He was the husband of Beatrice Dawson, of 10 Marshfield Place, Marshfield, Bradford, and sister of the late Francis Meek of 84 Glasgow St, Hull. He was killed in action on the 4th July 1917, aged 38. He is buried at Ridge Wood Military Cemetery, West Vlaanderen, Belgium.

2nd Lieutenant George Alan Webster of the 4th and 1st Battalion, East Yorkshire Regiment, was the son of George William and Eveline Rose Webster. The family home was 113 Westbourne Avenue. George married Louise Pretty (nee Webster), and they lived at 446a Anlaby Road. He was killed in action at Villers Guislain on 18th September 1918, aged 29. He is commemorated on the Vis-En-Artois Memorial, France.

Captain Thomas Mossop Clifford served with the Merchant Navy. He was the son of the late Thomas Atkinson Clifford and Emily Elizabeth Ann Clifford, and the husband of Sarah Eleanor Clifford, (nee Langstaff) of 22 Stirling Street. He was lost at sea on board *S.S. 'Cambric' (Hull)* through enemy action on the 31st October 1917, age 57. He is commemorated on the Tower Hill Memorial.

Able Seaman D/JX 313081 Fred Drewery served in the Royal Navy. He was the son of Fred and Henrietta Drewery of Hull. He was killed in action aboard *HMS President III on* the 26th March 1944. He is commemorated on the Plymouth Naval Memorial.

Private 9678 Cyril Eustace Mawer of the 2nd Battalion, East Yorkshire Regiment, was the son of Charles Henry and Annie Mawer, of 4 Adderbury Crescent, Beverley Road, and husband of Annie Eliza Mawer, of 4 Talbot Street, off Reed Street. He was killed in action at Ypres on the 4th February 1915, aged 32. He is commemorated on the Menin Gate Memorial, Ypres. He was the brother of **Private Charles Henry Mawer** who was accidentally killed at Curragh Camp, Ireland on the 27th November 1908.

Cadet Arthur John Sawney of The Royal Engineers, was the son of John and Mary Jane Sawney, 57 Albany Street, and was a student at Hymers College before the outbreak of war. He was accidentally drowned whilst training on the River Trent on the 16th December 1918, aged only 18. His body was recovered some time later, and a coroner's order was made on the 19th May 1919.

Fig.80. Arthur Sawney from his obituary notice.

2nd Lieutenant Stanley Clark served with the R.A.F., and was the son of George and Ann Clark, of Davenport Avenue, Hessle. He was killed in action at Hern-en-Artois, France, on the 17th September 1918, aged 26. He is buried in Pernes British Cemetery, near Calais.

Private 6711 Hubert Harry Elsom, 1/4th Battalion, King's Own Yorkshire Light Infantry, was the son of Albert and Emily Elsom, of 20 Gordon Street, Golden Square, London. The family were originally of Louis Street. He was killed in action in France on the 13th September 1916. He is buried at Lonsdale Cemetery, Authuille, Somme.

```
                                          Army Form B. 104—126.
    Any further letter on this
    subject should be addressed to    Station      Y O R K.
         Officer i/c
                     Records,         Date Sept 28th.    19 18.
    and the following No. quoted.

Mrs. E. Tommins,                      From The O.i/c No.1.
   15 Joshua Avenue,
        Madeley Street.                     Infantry Records,

Sir or Madam,  H U L L.                     Y O R K.
       I am directed to forward the undermentioned articles of
private property of the late No. 13 /1348 Rank    Pte.
Name           A. Swales.
Regiment 13th. Bn. East Yorkshire Regiment.
and would ask that you will kindly acknowledge receipt of the
same on the form overleaf:—

Wallet, letters, photos, 9 ct. Gold Ring,

knife, cards, (various) Confirmation

Certificate.


       These are the only articles at present forthcoming, but
should any further articles be received at any time they will be
duly forwarded.
                                  Yours faithfully
                                    11 OCT 1918

                                  for  Officer in charge of Records.
W182—M3048  250,000  10/17  HWV(cP139)   Forms B/104–126/1  No.1.York.
```

Fig.81. Letter informing next of kin of Alfred Swales' possessions at his death.

Private 11/1347 Alfred Alexander Tommins (Swales) of the 11th Battalion, East Yorkshire Regiment, was born in Hull in 1898, the son of Alfred and Emma Tommins. The family lived at 15 Joshua Terrace, Madeley Street. He worked as a compositor and attempted to join the Regiment in Hunslet when he was only 16, but was discharged as 'unlikely to become an efficient soldier'.

He changed his name to Swales, and tried again to enlist, this time successfully, in the East Yorkshire Regiment. He was killed by gunshot wounds to the chest and back on the 2nd July 1918, aged 20. He is buried in Longuenesse (St Omer) Souvenir Cemetery near Calais.

Civilian Casualties:

This book could never encompass the life stories, be they the small pen pictures we have used here in this work, of the civilian casualties that Hull lost in the two great conflicts of the twentieth century. The job becomes more manageable if we restrict the ones to be included simply to the ones buried in Hull General Cemetery, but even so we feel at our advanced ages, this is task best left to others, blessed with more energy.

However, there are two that justify inclusion. One, a man who, by virtue of his occupation, and because Michael Kelly, the Cemetery Superintendent, included him on his original list of war casualties in 1917 is included in this section. The second is a woman who by virtue of the circumstances of her death deserves a mention here.

In Michael Kelly's response to the Garrison letter (see Appendix 3), in which he was requested to identify all of the 'soldiers that had been buried in the war since 1914' he included one Arthur Twinton Dalton, who he listed as a telegraphist working for the North Eastern Railway.

Arthur Twinton Dalton was born in Hull, the son of Mr William and Mary Dalton, the family lived in Londesborough Street. He was employed as a telegraphist with the North Eastern Railway, and was living in Durham as a boarder in 1911. He died of double pneumonia in Sedgefield, Co. Durham on the 22nd June 1917 aged 41. His address at the time of his death was given as 105 Thoresby Street, Hull. Having checked all the available records, we can find no evidence of Arthur being in the armed forces, or find any reason for him being included for nomination for a war grave.

However, because his occupation was viewed as necessary to the war effort and therefore his job was a 'reserved occupation', it is likely that he was entitled to wear an armband with the message on it of 'On military service' or similar. In some way this allowed the person wearing such an emblem to not be threatened or abused by people demanding to know why they weren't serving in the armed forces.

Although not actually in military service at the time of his death Mr. Kelly probably made an honest mistake, in that as Arthur was conducting essential war work but was not enlisted in the forces he assumed he would warrant a war grave. The armed forces obviously thought differently on this matter.

There is one civilian woman casualty of enemy action, who is buried in the Hull General Cemetery. Although having no existing memorial we felt she should be memorialised in this book. **Alice Maud Hannah Gardam** was born in Beverley in 1862, the eldest daughter of Joseph and Catherine Gardam. Joseph was a licenced victualler in Wellington Lane on Beverley Road.

Her brother, Frederick John Gardam, became a solicitor, having a practice at 1 Parliament Street. In 1891 Alice was living in Victoria Avenue on her own means, but must have moved to Kensington sometime in the early 1900's. In the 1911 census, she is recorded as being in a private nursing home there. She apparently lived as companion to a Mrs Lindon, at 61 Warrington Crescent, Paddington, London, and on the evening of the 8th March 1918, the house was struck by a German bomb probably dropped from a Zeppelin. This disaster killed Mrs Lindon and Alice outright. The bodies were not recovered for some time, and a coroner's order was requested. Alice was buried in the family grave at Hull General Cemetery, however the headstone no longer exists.

Appendices

Appendix 1:

1a. IWGC Register of War Graves in Hull.

2a. IWGC Register of the War Graves in Hull General Cemetery.

THE WAR GRAVES OF THE BRITISH EMPIRE

The Register of the names of those who fell in the Great War and are buried in Hedon Road, Western, Northern, Old Hebrew Congregation, General and Holy Trinity (Hessle Road) Cemeteries, Hull, Sculcoates (Sacristy) Cemetery and Marfleet (St. Giles) Churchyard, Yorkshire

Compiled and Published by order of the Imperial War Graves Commission, London. 1926.

HULL GENERAL CEMETERY
CEMETERY INDEX NUMBER, YORKSHIRE 5

THIS cemetery, the property of a Company, adjoins Hull Western Cemetery. It was opened in 1847, and covers an area of about thirteen acres. It contains the scattered graves of ten soldiers from the United Kingdom and one sailor of the Royal Navy.

The Register records particulars of eleven British burials.

THE REGISTER OF THE GRAVES

BLACKBOURN, Pte. W. H., 21619. East Yorkshire Regt. 15th Nov., 1916. Son of Mrs. E. Blackbourn, of 91, Fish St., Hull. 709.

COBBY, Gnr. E., 104366. 12th Coy. Royal Garrison Artillery. 19th Feb., 1918. 10961.

COBBY, Lce. Cpl. W. H., TR/5/24218. 7th (Training Reserve) Bn. East Yorkshire Regt. 3rd Nov., 1916. Son of Mrs. M. A. Cobby, of 105, Spring Bank, Hull. 10961.

FARRELL, Lt. Adrian. 4th Bn. East Yorkshire Regt. 23rd Aug., 1916. Age 24. Son of Thomas Frederic and Monica Farrell, of 1, Brookside, Newland Park, Hull. 14150.

HODGSON, Armr. S/Serjt. J., T/1273. 130th (Light) Mobile Workshop, Royal Army Ordnance Corps. 15th June, 1920. Age 29. Husband of Nellie Hodgson, of 5, Berkley Terrace, Convent Lane, Anlaby Rd., Hull. 19148.

HOTCHKIN, Pte. William Henry, 3/6962. East Yorkshire Regt., transf. to (334137) Labour Corps. 9th March, 1918. Age 43. Son of William and Jane Hotchkin, of Hull; husband of Ada Wade Hotchkin, of 17, Ockley Terrace, West Parade, Hull. 8818.

JOHNSON, Maj. (Hon. Lt. Col.) Richard Ethelbert, V.D. General List, late East Riding, York, Royal Garrison Artillery. 29th Oct., 1915. Husband of Mrs. K. E. Johnson, of 49, Albany St., Hull. 26998.

KNOWLES, Lt. and Qmr. Vincent. Royal Engineers. 14th Oct., 1915 Age 53. Husband of Sarah Knowles, of 76, Blenheim St., Prince's Avenue, Hull. 10527.

MARR, Bmdr. A., 290044. 24th Siege Bty. Royal Garrison Artillery. 12th Nov., 1918. 15762.

SPENCE, Pte. G. F. W., 29530. 7th Bn. East Yorkshire Regt. 28th May, 1918. Age 19. Son of Fred Spence, of 21, Alexandra Rd., Hull. 11952.

WEST, Trimmer G., 6399 T.S. R.N.R. H.M.S. "Actaeon." 12th Nov., 1918. Husband of Mrs. A. West, of 73, Edgar St., Hessle Rd., Hull. 19538.

Appendix 2:

2a. IWGC Register of the War Graves in Hull General Cemetery with IWGC notations marked on it. Note the term 'unmaintainable'.

2b. As above of World War Two graves in the cemetery.

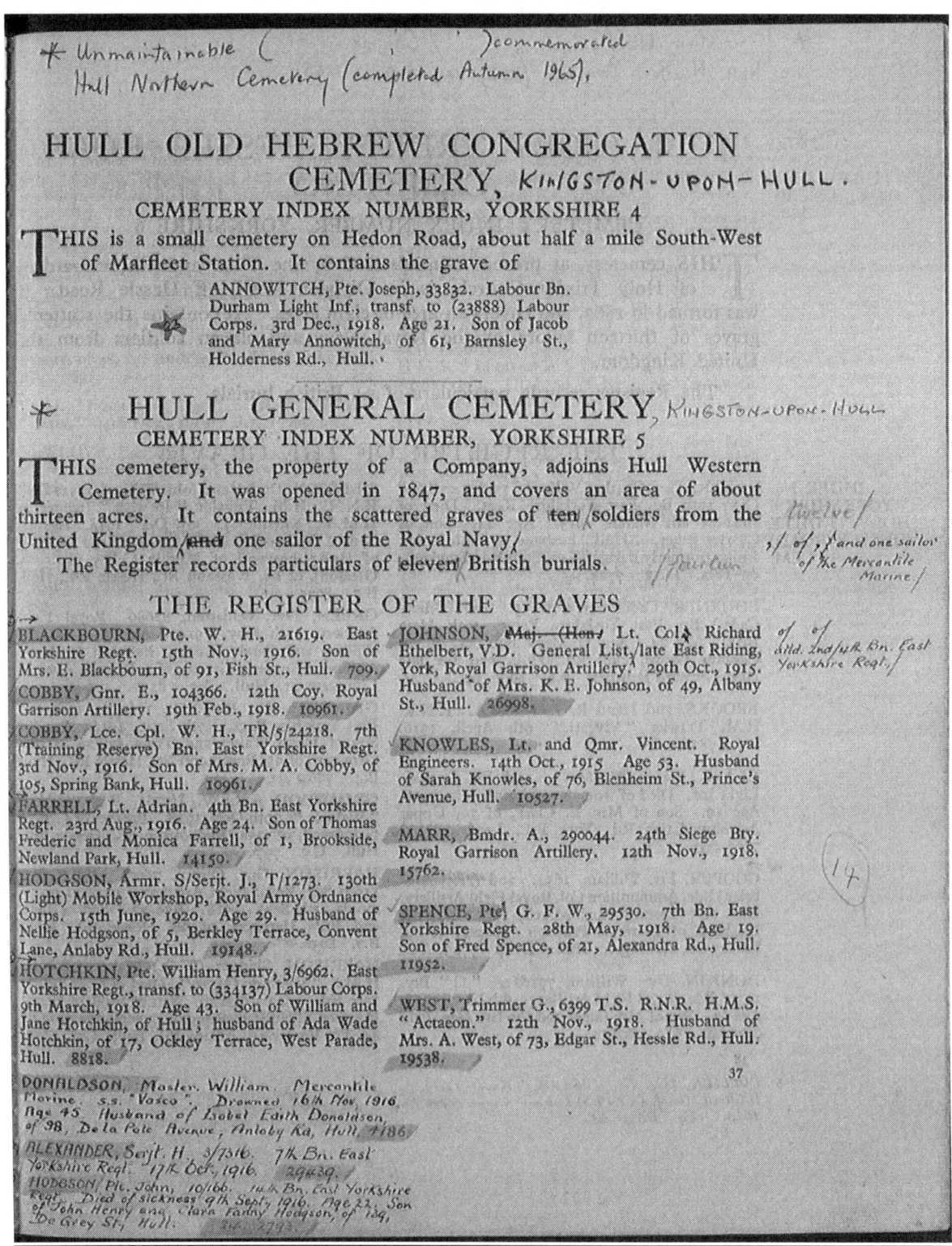

WHITE, A.C2 JAMES WILLIAM, 871022. R.A.F. (Aux. A.F.), 944 Balloon Sqdn. 18th March, 1945. Age 35. Son of William and Kate White, of Hull; husband of Mary Jane White. Compt. 317. Grave 80.

WILLARD, Ord. Sea. GORDON DENNIS, C/JX. 65194. R.N. 25th May, 1947. Age 21. Son of Thomas Randall Willard and Laura Cordelia Willard, of Hull. Compt. 130. Grave 8.

WILLCOX, Spr. JOHN ALBERT, 2017768. Royal Engineers. 14th March, 1946. Age 25. Son of Edward and Eliza Ann Willcox, of Hull. Compt. 255. Grave 27.

WILLIAMS, Flt. Sgt. FRANK, 759040. R.A.F. (V.R.), 228 Sqdn. 20th August, 1942. Age 22. Son of Alfred and Jane Williams, of Hull. Compt. 197. Grave 35.

WILSON, A.B. ARTHUR GILBERT, C/JX. 575539. R.N. H.M.S. Baldur. 26th June, 1946. Age 22. Son of Albert and Charlotte Ann Wilson, of Hull. Compt. 184. Grave 12.

WILSON, Dvr. G. W., T/292516. R.A.S.C. 1st April, 1947. Age 25. Son of Frederick and Amy Wilson, of Hull. Compt. 125. Grave 23.

WINDLE, A.C.1 JOHN WILLIAM MORGAN, 752073. R.A.F. (V.R.) 77 Sqdn. 15th August, 1940. Age 36. Son of John and Martha Alice Windle, of Hull; husband of Elizabeth May Windle, of Withernsea. Compt. 166. Grave 48.

WOOD, Tpr. JOHN (JACK), 7895429. 23rd Hussars, R.A.C. 25th July, 1944. Age 24. Son of Samuel and Caroline Wood, of Hull; husband of Alice Lorraine Wood, of Hull. Compt. 289. Grave 38.

WOOD, Sgt. (Pilot) ROBERT WALKER, R/106547. R.C.A.F. 31st March, 1943. Age 21. Son of Gladstone and Anne Elizabeth Wood, of Westminster, British Columbia, Canada. Compt. 225. Grave 17.

WOODFORD, Cpl. LEONARD, 1539488. R.A.F. (V.R.). 27th February, 1945. Age 23. Son of Thomas and Emma Woodford, of Hull; husband of Edna Elizabeth Woodford, of Hull. Compt. 202. Grave 61.

WRIGHT, A.C.1 CLIFFORD, 1102525. R.A.F. (V.R.). 31st December, 1941. Age 22. Son of Herbert and Hilda Wright, of Hull; husband of Mona Wright (née Clayton). Compt. 142. Grave 13.

WRIGHT, Cpl. JOHN EDWARD, D/26441. 6th (H.D.) Bn. The East Yorkshire Regt. 29th January, 1946. Age 43. Husband of Mary Elizabeth Wright, of Hull. Compt. 140. Grave 12.

HULL GENERAL CEMETERY, KINGSTON-UPON-HULL
(Index No. U.K. 1228)

BAKER, Sgt. (W. Op./Air Gnr.) FREDERICK CYRIL, 1073431. R.A.F. (V.R.). 29th December, 1941. Age 20. Son of Frances Baker, and stepson of John Morrison, of Hull. Grave 10825.

DUFF, A.C.2 (W. Op.) ERNEST, 552565. R.A.F. 9? Sqdn. 8th November, 1939. Grave 19336.

EVERS, Pte. HAROLD, 13028214. Aux. Mil. Pioneer Corps. 6th August, 1940. Grave 7844.

FARRELL, Maj. GILBERT VALENTINE, 107625, O.B.E. Pioneer Corps. 11th August, 1942. Age 58. Son of Thomas Frederick and Monica Collingwood Farrell, of Hull; husband of Dorothy Sherburn Farrell. Formerly served as Maj. with the 99th Deccan Infantry. Compt. 110. Grave 14326.

HARGREAVES, Pte. JAMES, D/22916. 6th (H.D.) Bn. The East Yorkshire Regt. 1st December, 1939. Age 50. Son of Joseph and Ann Hargreaves, of Hull. Grave 17066.

HUTTON, SYDNEY. Merchant Navy. Master, s.s. Albano (Hull). 2nd March, 1940. Age 51. Husband of M. E. Hutton, of Hull. Grave 5201.

KEMP, Pte. JOSEPH MUNDAY, 13088955. Pioneer Corps. 17th February, 1943. Age 32. Son of James Edward and Lily Kemp, of Hull; husband of May Kemp, of Hull. Grave 16021.

MARSTON, Boatswain FRANK. Merchant Navy. s.s. Somerby (London). 2nd October, 1947. Age 34. Son of Mr. and Mrs. Richard Baker Marston, of Hull; husband of Elsie May Marston, of Hull. Grave 18410.

MATHER, Pte. HARRY TREVOR, 14219902. The Durham Light Infantry. 20th February, 1944. Age 19. Son of George and Annie Mather, of Hull. Grave 12958.

MAWE, Fireman, PETER GEOFFREY. Naval Auxiliary Personnel (M.N.), H.M. Rescue Tug Griffin. 31st December, 1944. Son of Mr. and Mrs. A. W. Mawe, of Hull. Compt. 80. Grave 19940.

MEGGITT, A.C.2 OTTO FOWLER, 1025769. R.A.F. (V.R.). 31st March, 1941. Age 30. Son of Samuel and Ethel Jean Meggitt, of Willerby. Grave 3275.

ROBERTS, Ch. Engr. Off. ERNEST. Merchant Navy. s.s. Lorient (Cardiff). 4th April, 1942. Age 64. Son of John and Alys Roberts, of Southampton; husband of Eva Roberts, of Spring Bank, Hull. Grave 5226.

WOOD, Capt. GEORGE SHETLIFF, 46441. Royal Engineers. 16th February, 1944. Age 52. Son of Capt. George Edmund Wood, and of Lucy Wood, of Hessle; husband of Clara May Wood, of Fawley, Hampshire. Grave 2576.

WRIGGLESWORTH, Pte. ARTHUR, 4618082. The Duke of Wellington's Regt. (West Riding). 1st July, 1941. Grave 8615.

HULL (HEDON ROAD) CEMETERY, KINGSTON-UPON-HULL
(Index No. U.K. 1229)

This cemetery was severely damaged by enemy aircraft during the 1939-1945 War. In addition to the 93 burials recorded below, a memorial belonging to the Netherlands Merchant Navy is also erected here. The crematorium in which a number of service men and women were cremated is situated in this cemetery (see Index No. U.K. 1229A).
There are 205 burials of the 1914-1918 War and a Cross of Sacrifice erected near the entrance.

ATKINSON, Sto. 1st Cl. ALBERT, P/KX. D660. R.N. H.M.L.S.T. 299. 24th May, 1946. Age 25. Son of Albert Edward and Florence May Atkinson, of Hull; husband of Cora Atkinson, of Hull. Compt. 424. Grave 96.

CARTER, Dvr. HARRY, T/87547. R.A.S.C. 13th November, 1940. Age 18. Son of Mr. and Mrs. G. Carter, of Hull. Compt. 265. Grave 82.

COCHRANE, Pte. ERNEST, 13022858. Pioneer Corps. 5th April, 1941. Age 21. Son of Ernest Albert Verney Cochrane, and Elizabeth Ann Cochrane, of Hull. Compt. 429. Grave 47.

DENT, Spr. ALBERT, 2120651. Royal Engineers. 21st July, 1945. Age 55. Son of Johnston and Emily Dent, of Hull; husband of Doris Dent, of Hull. Compt. 241. Grave 45.

DICK, Pte. GEORGE VICTOR, S/65942. R.A.S.C. 26th January, 1942. Compt. 429. Grave 77.

DRY, L.A.C. WILLIAM, 1227370. R.A.F. (V.R.) 6th June, 1946. Age 37. Husband of Elsie Dry, of Hull. Compt. 392. Grave 46.

FENWICK, Sgt. (W. Op./Air Gnr.) ERNEST, 1075177. R.A.F. (V.R.). 7th May, 1943. Age 22. Son of Ernest and Violet Fenwick, of Hull. Compt. 378. Grave 96.

FITCHETT, Spr. LEONARD, 2000787. 9 Bomb Disposal Sec. Royal Engineers. 29th October, 1940. Age 23. Husband of Lottie Fitchett, of Stoneferry, Hull. Compt. 406. Grave 87.

HOGGARD, A.C.1 JOHN, 871725. R.A.F. (Aux. A.F.). 942/3 Balloon Sqdn. 3rd January, 1944. Husband of Harriet Hoggard, of Hull. Compt. 405. Grave 46.

HORSLEY, Bdr. HARRY, 865870. 15 Field Regt, Royal Artillery. 31st May, 1944. Age 24. Son of Harry and Selina Horsley, of Hessle. His brother John Robert also died on service. Compt. 430. Grave 7.

LAWSON, Spr. CHARLES EDWARD, 4281193. Royal Engineers. 19th February, 1944. Age 39. Husband of Evelyn Lawson, of Hull. Compt. 427. Grave 79.

LAZENBY, L. Bdr. HERBERT, 865087. 266 Bty., 82 H.A.A. Regt., Royal Artillery. 2nd February, 1946. Husband of F. Lazenby, of Moldgreen, Huddersfield. Compt. 393. Grave 60.

MALKIN, Seaman Cook JOHN WILLIAM, LT/JX. 179750. R.N. Patrol Service. H.M.S. Coventry City. 7th February, 1943. Age 39. Son of John Joseph and Diana Malkin, of Hull; husband of Ivy Malkin, of Hull. Compt. 10. Grave 29.

MONAGHAN, Pte. WILLIAM STEPHEN, 13004143. Pioneer Corps. 7th June, 1944. Compt. 434. Grave 33.

NEWEL, Ord. Coder ALEC, C/JX. 225490. R.N. H.M.S. Wallesley. 22nd November, 1940. Age 19. Son of Frank and Jessie Newel, of Hull. Compt. 426. Grave 93.

Appendix 3:

3a. Letter from IWGC to Hull General Cemetery, 1917, requesting details of the war dead buried in the cemetery.

3b. Hand written notes made by Michael Kelly in reply.

H.M. 9205

130, Anlaby Road,
Hull, 10/10/17

The Secretary,
    Hull General Cemetery Coy.,
        Hull.

[margin note: Army Council Instruction] A.C.I. 458 gives directions that the graves of every soldier who has died since the commencement of the War in 1914 up to the present date is to be suitably marked with a cross bearing his name, initials, and number, to be erected under the direction of the Royal Engineers.

This Army Council Instruction is only of recent date and though I have a record of every soldier who has died in Hull Hospitals I do not know the site of the grave in which his body is buried.

Would you please cause me to be furnished with this information and further whether there is any objection to the Commanding Royal Engineers sending a soldier into the Cemetery to affix the cross to each soldier's grave.

It is presumed that in your Cemetery Records you have a record of every soldier buried and the actual site and the number of the grave in which his body lies.

                                COLONEL,
                                A.D.M.S. HUMBER GARRISON.

Copy List furnished Military Authorities 11 Oct/17 — see Letter Book that date and as opposite.

An Officers & Soldiers buried in this Cem[etery]

Army No.	Name & any other particulars	Buried from	Date of Burial
10527	Viscount Knowles, Lieut. & Quartermaster, Royal Engineers	25 Morpeth St. Place	18 Oct. /15
14150	Adrian Farrell, Lieut. 4th Ey. Regt.	Queen Alexandra's Military Hospital, Millbank, London S.W.	25 Augt. /16
	Note — Parents have put a cross over grave		
2793	John Hodgson, Civil occupation only stated	Military Hospital, Withington Barracks, Litchford	12 Sept. /16
10961	Walter Harold Cobby, Civil occupation only stated	103 Springbank Hull	6 Nov. /16
	Note — Headstone already on grave with inscription in memory of deceased upon it		
18030	Thomas Roy Holden, Lock Flight Sub-Lieut. R.N.A.S.	Montpelier House, Lithobic Avenue, Bridlington	14 Nov. /16
	Note — Marble + already upon this grave —		
709	William Henry Blackborder, Civil occupation only stated	9 Peel St. Hull	19 Nov. /16
14194	Arthur Trueblood Dalton, Civil occupation (N.E.Ry Telegraphist) only stated	103 Thoresby St. Hull	22 June /17

Added later:—

10961	Cobby, Ernest	6 Granville St.	Feby 19th & 23rd 1918
26998	Johnson, Richard, Lithoid Stoker	409 Albany St.	Oct. 29 & Nov. 1 /18
8818	Hotchkin, Wm Hy, Private Soldier	17 Woolsey Terr. West Parade	Mch 9th & 14th /18

Appendix 4:

List of all the known graves in Hull General Cemetery.

Hull General Cemetery War Graves

Surname	Forenames	Regiment	Rank & No	Age	Died	Grave No
WW1						
Alexander	Herbert John	7th Battn East Yorks	Sgt 3/7316	41	17-10-1916	168/29439
Blackbourn	William Henry	East Yorks Regt	Pte 21619	22	15-11-1916	15/709
Cobby	Ernest	12th Company RGA	Gunner 104366	28	19-02-1918	83/10961
Cobby	Walter Harold	East Yorks Regt 7th Training Reserve	L/Cpl TR/5/24218	31	03-11-1916	83/10961
Donaldson	William	Mercantile Marine ss 'Vasco'	Master	35	16-11-1916	74/4186
Farrell	Adrian	4th Battn East Yorks	Lieut	24	23-08-1916	85/14150
Hodgson	John	130th (Light) Mobile Workshop RAOC	Armr sgt T/1273	29	15-06-1920	131/19148
Hodgson	John	14th Battn East Yorks	Pte 10/166	22	09-09-1916	24/2793
Hotchkin	William Henry	East Yorks Reg trans Labour Corps	Pte 3/6962 & 334137	43	09-03-1918	57/8818
Johnson	Richard Ethelbert	RGA, late East Yorks	Lieu Col	59	29-10-1915	159/26998
Knowles	Vincent	Royal Engineers	Lieut & Qtrmaster	53	14-10-1915	78/10527
Marr	Arthur	24th Seige Battery RGA	Brdr 290044	29	12-11-1918	110/15762
Spence	George F Walter	7th Battn East Yorks	Pte 29530	19	29-05-1918	82/11952
West	Gilbert	HMS 'Acteon'	Trimmer 6399 TS RNR	36	12-11-1918	130/19538
WW2						
Baker	Frederick Cyril	RAF (VR) Wireless Op Air Gunner	Sgt 1073431	20	28-12-1941	79/10925
Duff	Ernest	RAF 97 Sqdn Wireless Operator	AC2 552565	18	08-11-1939	131/19316
Evers	Harold	Auxilliary Mil Pioneer Corps	Pte 13028214	34	06-08-1940	58/7844
Farrell	Gilbert Valentine	Pioneer Corps formerly 99th Inf Indian	Major 107625 (OBE)	58	11-08-1942	110/14326
Hargreaves	James	6th(HD) Battery East Yorks	Pte D/22916	49	01-12-1939	118/17066
Hutton	Sydney	Merchant Navy ss 'Albano'	Mariner	51	02-03-1940	38/5201
Kemp	Joseph Mundy	Pioneer Corps	Pte 13088955	32	17-02-1943	117/16621
Marston	Frank	Merchant Navy ss 'Samsteel' (London)	Boatswain	34	02-10-1947	81/9990
Mather	Harry Trevor	Durham Light Infantry	Pte 14219902	19	20-02-1944	83/12938
Mawe	Peter Geoffrey	Naval Aux Personnel HM Tug 'Griffin'	Fireman	20	31-12-1944	81/9990
Meggitt	Otto Fowler	RAF (VR)	AC2 1025789	30	31-03-1941	82/3275
Roberts	Ernest	Merchant Navy ss 'Lorient' (Cardiff)	Chief Eng	59	04-04-1942	41/5226
Wood	George Shetliff	Royal Engineers	Capt 46441	52	16-02-1944	38/2576
Wrigglesworth	Arthur	Duke of Wellington's Regt (West Riding)	Pte 4618983	22	01-07-1941	58/8615

Appendix 5:

Map of the Hull General Cemetery with the known CWGC graves marked.

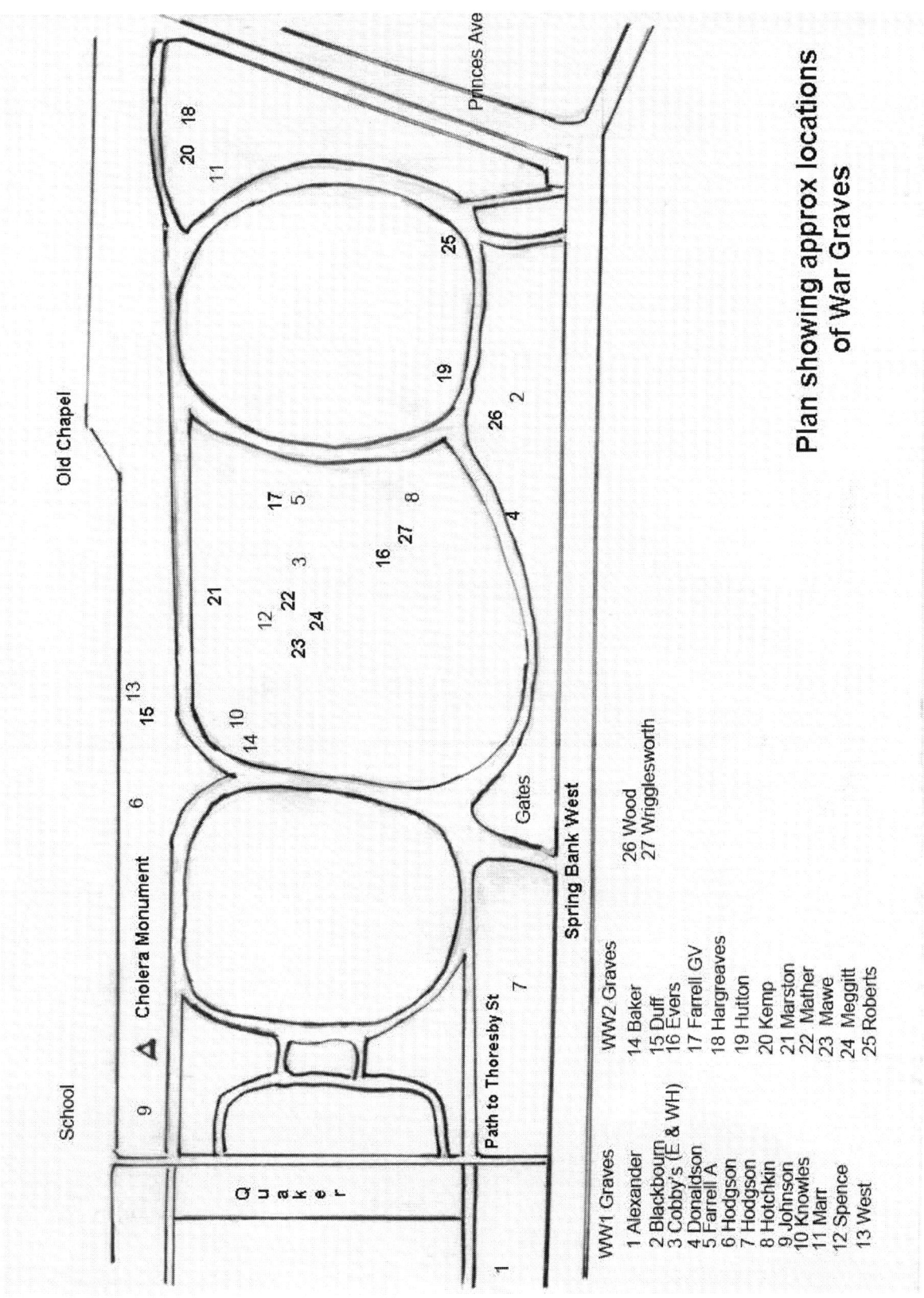

Appendix 6:

Images of the Panels in Northern Cemetery that replaced the War Graves of Hull General Cemetery.

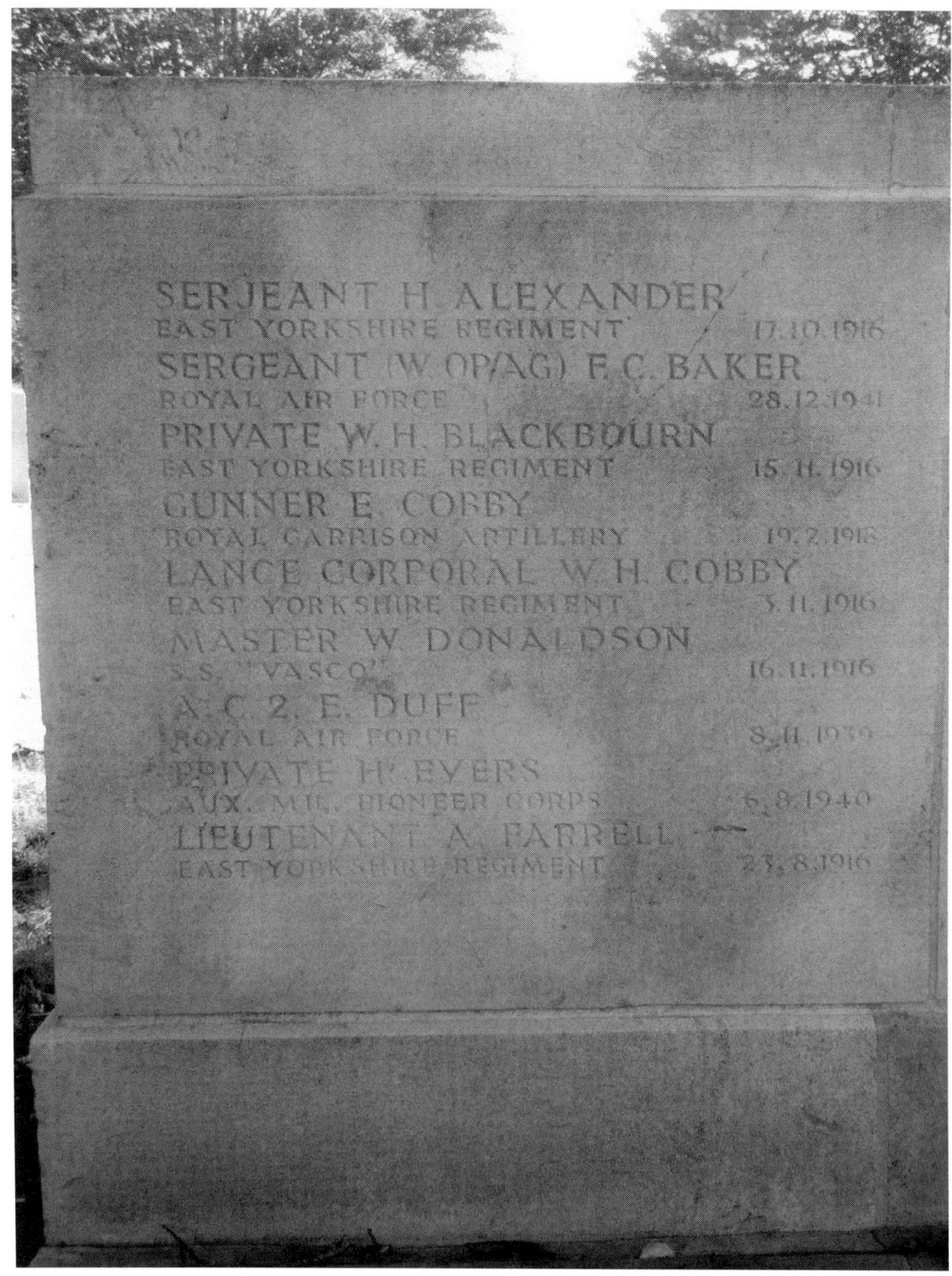

Bibliography

Articles:

'The Commonwealth War Graves Commission', Peter Francis, Head of External Communications – Commonwealth War Graves Commission, in **The Family and Local History Handbook 8**, Ed: Robert Blatchford, Robert Blatchford Publishing Ltd., 2007.

'How the Unknown Warrior Came Home at Last', David Barnes, in **The Family and Local History Handbook 12**, Eds: Robert and Elizabeth Blatchford, Robert Blatchford Publishing Ltd., 2011.

'Remembering the Fallen', Peter Francis, Head of External Communications – Commonwealth War Graves Commission, in **The Family and Local History Handbook 13**, Eds: Robert and Elizabeth Blatchford, Robert Blatchford Publishing Ltd., 2012.

'How You Can Help Preserve the Nation's War Memorials', Frances Moreton, Director – War Memorials Trust, in **The Family and Local History Handbook 14**, Eds: Robert and Elizabeth Blatchford, Robert Blatchford Publishing Ltd., 2013.

Books:

1914-1918, David Stevenson, Penguin, 2004.

A History of Hull, Edward Gillett & Kenneth A. MacMahon, The University of Hull Press, 1989.

Boy Soldiers of the Great War, Richard Van Emden, Headline Book Publishing, 2005.

British and Commonwealth War Cemeteries, Julie Summers, Shire, 2010.

British Postcards of the First World War, Peter Doyle, Shire, 2011.

Courage Remembered, T.A. Edwin Gibson & G.Kingsley Ward, HMSO, 1989.

Death in England, Eds. Peter C. Jupp & Clare Gittings, Rutgers University Press, 1999.

Death in War and Peace, Pat Jalland, Oxford University Press, 2010.

Empires of the Dead, David Crane, Harper Collins, 2013.

History of the First World War, Basil Liddell Hart, Pan Books, 1972.

Hull & The Humber: Remembering 1914-18, Susanna O'Neill, The History Press, 2015.

Hull Commercials, Ed. David Bilton, Pen & Sword, 2018.

Humberside in the First World War, Stephen Kimberley, Local History Archives Unit, 1988.

Keep the Home Fires Burning, Ed. John Markham, Highgate, 1988.

Known to the Night, B.S. Barnes, Sentinel Press, 2002.

Known Unto God, B.S. Barnes, Sentinel Press, 2013.

Lost Churches and Chapels of Hull, David Neave, Hutton Press, 1991

Mud, Blood and Poppycock, Gordon Corrigan, Cassell, 2003.

Peacemakers; Six months that Changed the World, Margaret Macmillan, John Murray, 2001

Poems of the First World War, Ed. Martin Stephenson, Everyman Edition, 1993.

Poetry of the First World War, J.M. Gregson, Edward Arnold, 1976.

Remembering Hull in the Great War, Simon Dinsdale, Horsley & Dawson, 2013

Singled Out, Virginia Nicholson, Penguin, 2007.

Six Weeks, John Lewis-Stempel, Orion, 2010

Soldiers Died In The Great War 1914-1919: The East Yorkshire Regiment, War Office, J.B. Hayward & Son, 1989.

The Decline and Fall of the British Empire:1781-1997, Piers Brendon, Jonathon Cape, 2007.

The Fateful Year: England 1914, Mark Bostridge, Penguin, 2014.

The First Gun Shots of the Great War: Hull Men at the Front in 1914-15, Simon Dinsdale, Amadeus Press, 2015.

The First World War, Hew Strachan, Pocket Books, 2003

The Imperial War Museum Book of the Western Front, Malcolm Brown, Pan Books, 1993.

The Last Post, Max Arthur, Phoenix Press, 2005.

The Myth of the Great War, John Mosier, Profile Books, 2001.

The Penguin Book of First World War Poetry, Ed. Jon Silkin, Penguin, 1981.

The Quick and the Dead, Richard Van Emden, Bloomsbury, 2011.

The Road Home, Max Arthur, Phoenix Press, 2009.

The Soldier's War, Richard Van Emden, Bloomsbury, 2008.

The Story of 25 Eventful Years in Pictures, Odhams Press, 1935.

The Telegraph Book of Readers' Letters from the Great War, Ed. Gavin Fuller, Aurum Press, 2014.

The Trench: The Full Story of the 1st Hull Pals, David Bilton, Pen & Sword, 2002.

The Unending Vigil, Philip Longworth, Pen & Sword, 2003.

The Viking Atlas of World War 1, Anthony Livesey, Penguin Books, 1994.

The Western Front, Marcel Belley, Uniform Publishing Group, 2017.

The Work of the Dead, Thomas W. Laqueur, Princetown University Press, 2015.

The World's War, David Olusoga, Head of Zeus Ltd., 2014.

The World War One Source Book, Philip J. Haythornthwaite, Brockhampton Press, 1992.

This Righteous War, B.S. Barnes, Richard Netherwood Ltd., 1990.

Till The Boys Come Home, Tonie & Valmai Holt, Macdonald & Jane's Publishers Ltd., 1977.

Up The Line To Death, Ed. Brian Gardner, Magnum Books, 1980.

War Memorials in Britain, Jim Corke, Shire Publications, 2005.

Warrior Race, Lawrence James, Abacus, 2001.

Printed in Poland
by Amazon Fulfillment
Poland Sp. z o.o., Wrocław